A War With No Name:
Post Traumatic Stress Disorder, a suvivors story

ISBN 1-58898-931-3

A War With No Name:
Post Traumatic Stress Disorder, a suvivors story

Dr. Art Schmitt
CDR USN RETIRED

greatunpublished.com
Title No. 931
2003

A War With No Name:

Post Traumatic Stress Disorder, a suvivors story

TABLE OF CONTENTS

ACKNOWLEDGEMENTS

I would like to take this opportunity to give a special thanks to my wife, Marilyn, who patiently stood by over the years as I labored over this manuscript and tried to get everything perfect. I would also like to thank my editors who made it possible to get things in order and help the book to come to fruition. Thanks also to Tom Klavon, AO-3, one of my wonderful door gunners, who supplied me with some great photos for this book and who saved my butt on more than one occasion. I would be remiss if I didn't give tribute to my number two man, the pilots, the fire team leaders, all of the door gunners, and the maintenance guys in all of my squadrons who made this story possible. Finally, I would like to thank Rear Admiral Kevin Delaney for his unwavering support from the days we flew together through today, as I now bring this book to press. Because of Admiral Delaney and Chief Petty Officer Rutledge, I was awarded a Distinguished Flying Cross—32 years after the fact—on September 17, 2002. The medal will be officially awarded to me in Charleston at the HAL-3 reunion in 2004.

Dr. Art Schmitt

In the later part of 1970, I was selected as HAL-3 Det. 1 Petty Officer in Charge. Upon my arrival, the camaraderie of both enlisted and officer ranks impressed me, as this does not just happen, but rather takes good leadership. Art Schmitt was the Commanding Officer and, in my estimation, he was an outstanding officer and human being. He led by example, whether on the ground or in the air, and expected the same from his subordinates. The bathroom we used was an outhouse with half barrels in the underside. When they became partially full, they had to be pulled out and burned with diesel fuel until empty, which entailed a lot of stirring with a stick and trying to stay down wind from the smoke and smell. This job was not below Cdr. Schmitt as he took his rotation on this unpleasant task; such was his dedication and exemplary commitment to duty. I flew over 600 combat missions and am proud to have served with a man of Cdr. Schmitt's caliber. Read and enjoy this brave man's experiences.

Fred T. Stark AOCS (CAC)
U.S. Navy Retired

In the summer of 1970, I had the privilege of joining Detachment One of the United States Navy Sea Wolves (HAL-3) in the Mekong Delta of South Vietnam. At that time, Dr. Art Schmitt was the commanding officer and was known as Cdr. Art Schmitt (or "Uncle Art"). Little did I know how fortunate I would be to serve under his leadership in this truly unique fighting force of sailors. All established methods of command had to be rewritten in order to earn the respect of these seasoned combat veterans. Cdr. Schmitt led by example, always there at the front, allowing his men to do their jobs to the best of their ability by giving them the same respect as everyone else in our team. On every mission the possibility of disaster lurked. The mental strain on us was tremendous, yet there was never the slightest problem manning those gunships, no matter how great the odds were against us. I flew 853 combat missions and Cdr. Schmitt is, without a doubt, the best officer I ever served under. His experiences are truly documented in *A War with No Name*.

Michael W. Dobson
Aviation Electricians Mate 2nd Class (AE2)

United States Navy Commander Art Schmitt is a true American hero, legend and warrior. He was respectfully nicknamed "Uncle Art" by his sailors in South Vietnam. In 1970, Commander Schmitt was the "Officer in Charge" of HAL-3, Detachment 1, which was located deep in the Vietcong strongholds of South Vietnam. Commander Schmitt's leadership style was simply to lead from the front and never ask his sailors to do anything he wouldn't do or hadn't done. Commander Schmitt was a "top gun" leader and helicopter pilot who had the well-deserved reputation of taking care of his gunners and pilots. Commander Schmitt never left friendly troops in harm's way and never refused a mission, no matter how dangerous. He brought all of his sailors home, and, after thirty years, I would like to say thank you, Commander Schmitt, for bringing *me* home. *A War With No Name* is a compelling story, a must read about the legendary Sea Wolf helicopter gunships and their special missions.

Tom Olby
Det.1

A lot of water has passed under the proverbial bridge since Vietnam, but always in the forefront of my mind are the memories of serving as a door gunner with the Sea Wolves on Det-1. This is a testimony to the greatness of all who served with HAL-3, especially to Art Schmitt, CO Det-1. The US Navy has produced many fine aviators, but Art was one of those people who excelled in bringing the best out of all of us. We were willing to go the extra mile because he was there, no matter how hairy the missions became. The ever-present threat of disaster was always trying to rear its ugly head, but we all faced it head on with our skipper leading by example. The hazards were great, the risks high, and the decisions and pressures the Officer in Charge had to endure were profound; Art, however, remained focused and determined throughout the war. Great leadership allows talents to rise, and they did under his tenure. His ear was always tuned to his men for ideas, wisdom, and the experiences of other servicemen. That is one of the main reasons Det-1 became a most potent and feared fire team in the Delta, as well as trusted by all who called upon us for our skills. Whatever it took to complete the mission, it was done. We all became brothers, brothers who could be called upon to cover each other's backsides, and it all starts with great leadership. Art, thanks for getting my butt back time and time again!

Tom Klavon
AO-3

For my late parents, Catherine and Arthur Schmitt Sr., who never stood in the way of my dreams, but rather extended their full and unwavering support and encouragement in everything I did—including flying.

.

INTRODUCTION

This book is about the many experiences in my career as a Naval Aviator and in particular, as I have discussed, my three tours in Vietnam and how they affected my life after Nam. Perhaps my training in Psychology or just my common sense enabled me to develop coping skill to deal with my Post Traumatic Disorder. I have related the stories that helped to create the disorder in my mind. There have been various techniques I have used over the years to alleviate the symptoms and cope with the stress. Many times I have had tinges and, most recently since moving to the South, I have experienced transformations of the marshes turning into rice patties before my eyes.

In appendix one I discussed PTSD as I experienced it. In addition to my comments, one of my door gunners who suffer from PTSD, feels that the root cause of the trauma must be located and treated. Taking responsibility is only then applicable when the source is found. He goes on to explain that once the patient has been made fully cognizant of the cause, and accepts that cause, only then can he or she take the responsibility necessary to implement change.

FOREWORD

I was honored to be asked by my good friend, Commander Art Schmitt, to write the foreword to his book, *A War With No Name*. As you will learn from reading this book, Art was a hero in war. He answered the call to the service of our great country very early in his life, and he subsequently completed three combat tours in Vietnam. He did so willingly while many others shirked from the responsibility. Now, by openly relating his own personal struggles with Post-Traumatic Stress Syndrome, Art has once again become a hero, and he has done so in peacetime. I most sincerely wish that his candor will provide solace and hope for all who suffer from this very real affliction, as well as to their family members who have stood by during so many difficult times and circumstances.

Art's story is a real one. Many of his stories brought back for me memories long forgotten. To those of us young officers who found ourselves in the heat of battle literally weeks after being designated as new Navy Aviators, "Uncle Art" was a source of great strength, stability and trust. Of the 125 or so pilots in our squadron, over 100 were serving in their very first duty assignment. We were about as "green" as one could possibly be, and yet we had to grow up very fast if we were to survive. Uncle Art took so many of us under his wing and showed us the ropes. He was a great mentor, leader and role model for us all. I was proud to call him my friend then, as I am proud to call him my friend now. This is his story.

Rear Admiral Kevin Delaney

That strange feeling we had in the war. Have you found anything in your lives since equal its strength? A sort of splendid carelessness it was, holding us together-"

Noel Coward

This book is dedicated to the men and women who lost their lives, limbs and souls in the Vietnam conflict. They served their country with courage and valor while experiencing the horror and pains of a war that was, from the beginning, not meant to be—truly "A War With No Name." I salute those individuals who died as well as those who returned home carrying in their minds the unendurable visions of war, only to receive disdain and suspicion from their countrymen, rather than the respect and admiration veterans of past wars have enjoyed. After a number of years an attempt was made to honor our fallen heroes by erecting a wall in Washington, D.C. where the 58,266 names of those lost would be inscribed for all to read. It is appropriate that this monument today is hidden from view, set off from any road in the middle of a large park, since the fact that these men and women were in Vietnam was also hidden for a long time from the public eye. (Only recently have figures of soldiers been added to the monument so that it can be easily located.) Many of us returned home suffering from a condition known as Posttraumatic Stress Disorder (PTSD), a topic I take on in this book. Those who have chosen to overcome this disorder have had to fight another long and unnecessary battle. This book is especially for them.

Dr. Art Schmitt
CDR Art Schmitt, USN Retired

CHAPTER ONE

I was 15 years old and visiting a girlfriend at her parents' lake house in New Jersey, when an airplane flew over at an altitude of about 300 feet. As I watched the F4-U swoop down low over the lake and disappear on the horizon, every bone in my body vibrated and my spine tingled with excitement. It was at that moment I knew I wanted to be a pilot. From that day forward, I started planning to get my various aircraft licenses. Shortly after the incident at the lake, I found out that I had a heart murmur and might not be able to qualify physically to get into a flight-training program. The disappointment I felt with that news was devastating.

As a youth I was very active in the Boy Scouts of America, and at the age of 16, I was selected as the Honor Eagle Scout of the Year for New York City. The authorities asked me what I wanted to do in honor of this award; I shot for the moon, literally, and told them I wanted to fly in a jet. The year was 1952 and there weren't a lot of jets flying around, so it took them almost a year to honor my request. When I was 17, an Air Force vehicle with a two-star flag on the side showed up at my parents' apartment in Brooklyn. The General's vehicle drove me to Mitchell Air Force Base on Long Island. There I met a Korean Jet Fighter Pilot Ace who escorted me to the General's B-25, a WWII bomber that was very small but plush inside. They flew me to Suffolk Country Air Force Base where I met another Korean pilot. He gave me a safety briefing and then strapped me into an aircraft seat that was attached to rails pointed at an angle toward the sky. This was an ejection seat trainer. I put my helmet on, secured my goggles, and waited for the blast. They instructed me to pull the trigger and bang! Two cannon shells went off and I flew up the rails and abruptly stopped where they ended. It was as close as you could get to ejecting from a jet without really doing so. I hoped my flight a few minutes later would not culminate in an ejection over New York City.

I climbed into a T-33 jet with two tandem seats and we taxied out to the runway for what would be the thrill of my young life. We flew over the city. I had never experienced the joy and elation that looking down at my home city gave me. As we climbed to altitude, I knew that I had to become a pilot to slip the surly bonds of earth and touch the face of God. In my excitement, I forgot that I had to go to the bathroom. I asked the pilot if there was anything that I could do, and he said, "Under your seat is a relief tube and you can do it that way." There I was, at 36,000 feet, pissing on New York. We landed and the General's car whisked me away to the Officers' Club, where I had lunch with the General and the two pilots. Realizing it wouldn't be long before I'd be back in the real world, where I wouldn't have Generals holding doors for me and asking me to lunch, I grinned to myself. The thought left me longing even more for a career in aviation.

As the years went on, I studied everything I could about aviation and tried to scrounge a ride any chance I could. I read every book I could find on aviation, and saw any movie that featured flying (I specifically recall enjoying *The Bridges at Toko-Ri*). I hung around the Navy base in Brooklyn, Floyd Bennet Field, and Idlewild Airport on Long Island. I used to take the bus or train to these locations just so I could hang around and watch the planes. Eventually, I met a couple of guys at general aviation who would take me flying. It was getting in my blood; that I could feel.

I figured the best way to get my licenses was to go into a military program and get assigned to multi-engine aircraft. It would be considerably cheaper than going the civilian route and paying for training and flight time. It would save me a fortune, and the only catch would be a small obligation of military service. This led me to the Air Force program, because I knew that I had a better chance of getting the multi-engine training that would qualify me for the airlines. I found out that the Navy tests to enter flight training were harder. I had thought that I would cut my teeth on those tests. There were, in fact, a number of psychological and academic tests required for both services. Speaking with the recruiters and anyone else who had some data on the tests, I researched the situation. They all informed me that there was no real way to study for these tests. All the necessary knowledge had to already be in your brain.

When it was time to go to college, I took engineering subjects to prepare myself for the technical aspects of flight training and ground school. However, I found that I made better grades in psychology and sociology than I did in the engineering subjects, which would later play an important part in my adult life. Finally, after two years of junior college, I had amassed enough college credits to get into either the Navy or the Air Force flight-training program. I took the Navy tests first and passed them, so I thought I would take my chances with the Navy program and see if I could get into the multi-engine program instead of taking the Air Force tests. My plan was to get my wings of gold that signify having the requisite flight time and knowledge to be an airline pilot. The day that I took the physical a miracle occurred: my heart murmur was gone and I easily passed all the tests. At 18 years old, I reported to Pensacola on June 30, 1955 to begin my flying career.

During my initial phase of flight training I was selected for the Naval Aviation Cadet Drill Team. Of the cadets selected, only 48 would march in any football game. We were carefully screened for attitude, aptitude and the ability to squeeze six days of ground school into three days, while marching at the quick pace of 120 steps per minute and spinning a rifle. Our mission was to fly out of the base on a Thursday, party at some university on the other side of the country, practice Saturday morning, and march in a football game at half time. It was exciting traveling across the United States to watch some of the greatest games of the season. We performed once in the Orange Bowl. The experience was terrifying; I dropped my rifle and

88,000 people went "Aw!" We were assigned an Ensign as our public information officer. He would go to a city a week before our arrival and put together incredible events. Once such event was a tea dance at the Colorado Women's College in Denver. When we arrived, there were 450 girls to our 77 cadets. We mingled with the girls, had a ball, and picked the girl or girls we wanted to go out with. At one of the schools, we sat in the back of convertibles with the Queen and her court and rode through town in the pre-game parade. At another college, we were split up into groups of four cadets and dined at separate sorority houses. Yes, this was the way man was meant to live!

We would normally wet our gloves so we could properly grip the rifles when we spun them. However, on a visit to the University of Minnesota, the temperature was 19 degrees, so we couldn't use the gloves; luckily this time no one dropped their rifles. All in all, it was a wonderful football season and we had a grand time marching and partying. We got through the season with a horrendously busy schedule and we all graduated from preflight.

Obviously, I was still fixated on becoming an airline pilot, so when the opportunity arose, I jumped at getting into multi-engine training. I was stationed at Barin Field in Alabama, where I was preparing to learn how to land on an aircraft carrier when they asked for volunteers to go to Hutchison, Kansas to fly multi-engines. Apparently, the Navy was short on multi-engine pilots. We skipped career qualifications and were immediately whisked off to Kansas. Beechcraft, a twin reciprocating engine aircraft, and later P2V's, also with two reciprocating engines, were my training aircraft at this time. I finished flight training and was designated a Naval Aviator on December 13, 1956.

Soon after flight training I was assigned to an Anti Submarine Squadron in Quonset Point, Rhode Island. We deployed to Argentia, Newfoundland and flew ice patrols to Iceland, Greenland and Labrador, as well as making frequent trips up Bafin Bay to Saunderstrom and Thule. We did this tour for 5 months each year for four long years. Our ice observer would sit in the nose, look down, and say, "The ice will break on the 13th of July." Sure enough, when we came back on July 13, the ice would be cracking. We had to fly to a radar site 780 miles from the North Pole and drop mail. After we got up there and finished our mission, I told the crew, "Let's go all the way to the pole." The navigator had to use polar navigation because we were too close to the magnetic pole and the compasses weren't working properly. We flew for 3 ½ hours and the navigator said we were there. When I banked the plane, we all looked down, saw nothing but desolation, and flew home.

We also went to Europe, on occasion, on what they called European familiarizations or Eur-fams. On one Eur-fam, we went to Paris and toured a perfume factory downtown. We were seated in very low, comfortable chairs behind a bar, when gorgeous models came by, leaned over and said, "This is odor of arm pit," or something along those lines. Then they gave us each a glass of brandy. The bottom line was, we never saw the Eiffel tower, spent three days in the perfume factory, and pissed away $800 on perfume and other things. What a trip!

After that tour, I tried to get out of the Navy and become an airline pilot, but companies weren't hiring. So I stayed in and was sent to Pensacola to become a flight instructor in T-28's, a single-engine tandem seat plane with tricycle landing gear. I spent the next four years flying, and I eventually wound up with 1900 hours in that wonderful aircraft.

About two and a half years into this assignment, they were short on flight students, so they gave the guys who hadn't had the opportunity to get carrier qualified a chance to do so. Though I had amassed nearly 1500 hours in the T-28 by this point, I did not have a lot of formation flying experience. A few weeks before the date I was scheduled to go back to Barin Field to fly field carrier-landing practices, I practiced slow flight, which means having the canopy open, gear and flaps down, and approaching at a speed just above stall speed. This is the configuration used to land on a ship. By this time, I had almost eight years in the Navy but had never landed on an aircraft carrier-the signature maneuver of a Naval Aviator. To my chagrin, I was not a full-fledged tail hooker. Finally the day came for the spectacular event. We were briefed that we would fly in a formation of 8 T-28's out to the USS Lexington in the Gulf of Mexico, a few miles off Pensacola. The first pass would be at 200 feet just to get the feel of looking at the postage stamp-sized target we were about to land on. The next two passes were to be touch and goes, with no hook. The next eight would be arrested with the hook down. We were instructed to pull our shoulder straps down as hard as we could stand it, because when the aircraft touched down and the hook caught the wire, our faces would come about two inches from the instrument panel. We were also instructed to add full power when we touched down, just in case the hook didn't grab, so we could take it around. We didn't want to be with no power if we hadn't grabbed the hook. There were six wires in those days, so, depending on how good you were, if you didn't hit the middle one you had five other options.

We suited up and took off in a formation of 8 T-28's, I was fourth in the pack, and flew out to the ship. Having a hell of a time flying formation, that is, trying to keep from colliding with the other aircraft, I was adding power, pulling power off, and dropping the speed brakes so that I wouldn't have a mid-air with my flight team members. We made it out to the ship, and I was right, it looked like a postage stamp. We broke one at a time, and I proceeded to do my fly by at 200 feet. The Landing Signal Officer (LSO) started screaming at me, "You can't land on the ship at that altitude!" I thought back to my briefing just an hour before: the first pass was supposed to be a fly by. After the LSO scolded me sufficiently, I proceeded to do my touch and goes. I made my first touch and go, and the LSO starting screaming at me again. "Your hook isn't down!" I was doing exactly as we were briefed. What was wrong with this picture? I was really rattled, wasn't thinking right, and as a result I was all over the sky. Each and every landing the LSO yelled at me at the top of his lungs, "You are too low, you are too high!" I never hit the same wire twice, and my face came within inches of the instrument panel as my shoulder straps strained to keep me in place. When I finished my eight carrier landings or "traps," as they were called, I breathed a sigh of relief.

We flew back and I was exhausted. When the seven other pilots walked over to my aircraft, they were in uproarious laughter. As they approached, I could see that they were instructors for the FCLP group. They had set me up to get me rattled and lose my self-confidence. I laughed with them, and was aggravated by their prank, but at least I was finally a real naval aviator! Little did I know that I was going to make the Navy my career and would amass 500 more carrier landings (including about 200 at night and some on a pitching career deck).

At the end of four years the airlines were still not hiring, so again I stayed in. Washington called and told me that they wanted to send me to a ship as an assistant air boss or assistant hangar deck officer. When I told the detailer that I didn't want to be on a ship, he said, "Well you are in the Navy, you know." They then told me that they were short of helicopter pilots, so I transitioned to helos, and they promptly sent me to a squadron that deployed on the USS Yorktown (CVS-10, now a museum one mile from my house here in Charleston, SC).

The War With No Name began for me in the winter of 1964. My squadron was stationed aboard the Yorktown CVS-10, the second Yorktown (the first was sunk in the second World War at the battle of Midway). We were sailing to the Far East, and this was my first trip to that part of the world. It was also my first time aboard a crowded, smelly aircraft carrier. We were not happy with the idea of being away from our families for 5 months. Because of a small skirmish in Southeast Asia that would soon become the Vietnam War, it would turn out to be nine months. Though we already missed home, we were looking forward to visiting the Far East and doing a little sightseeing in the great land of rice and shopping malls.

We were steaming toward Hong Kong when the bullhorn (our ship's communication address system) sounded with an announcement. The Captain informed us that there was a small conflict brewing in Southeast Asia but we were not to be concerned, as it would only affect us because of our proximity to the fighting. He assured us, in no simple terms, that we were still going to Hong Kong to party, so we continued on our way. A few days later, the bullhorn lit up again and an announcement was made that we would not be going to Hong Kong after all, but instead would be heading to waters off the coast of Vietnam in the South China Sea. My roommates and I looked at each other and we all had the same sinking feeling in our stomach. We pulled out our maps and tried to locate Vietnam. It was an obscure country that none of us really knew anything about. The captain told us not to worry, that this was only an internal conflict and that we would not get involved. We would never see the coast, let alone land on terra firma.

While at sea, I applied for, and was selected to participate in, Officer of the Deck Under Way training. The training was intense, and the Captain of the ship selected only three squadron pilots to undergo the training. In addition to watching the bridges, one of the responsibilities of Deck Officers, we were assigned to other individual duties. Mine was Maintenance Officer for 16 helos, as well as flying our regularly scheduled sorties into North Vietnam. A typical day went like this: Wake up at 4:00 a.m. to stand a bridge watch for four hours, go to the office for our day job, fly a five hour hop in the evening (either as plane guard alongside the ship or as an escort for the fighters and bombers making constant runs into Vietnam), then finally sleep for a few hours until we were required back on the bridge. We did this for 90 days.

Our training required knowing every inch of the ship, forward and back, by the end of the 3 months. We had to take a 4-hour written exam and a 3-hour oral exam administered by the Captain and 3 other OD's (Officers of the Deck Under Way). I passed the exams with flying colors and was bestowed the prestigious honor of being designated a Qualified Officer of the Deck Under Way-the only squadron officer with that qualification.

My first bridge watch occurred while going into Tokyo harbor. Fortunately, the Captain was on deck because the boat and ship traffic were unbelievably tight. There were watercrafts of all kinds: tiny one-man fishing boats, small and large sailboats, tugboats, and huge steam ships. However, nothing there was as big as the Yorktown, which measures about 1,000 feet long. In the early light of dawn, it looked like a few of these vessels were headed straight for us or were sitting directly in our path. Actually, some of them were. Whenever a vessel was closer than 1,000 yards, the Captain had to be called to the bridge. At first, I had the con as we entered Tokyo Bay, but in a matter of minutes, the traffic increased 4-fold, and the Captain was called up. It seemed like hours passed while I waited for the Captain to get there. In the minutes before his arrival, I guided the massive ship into the harbor. Soon the Captain arrived on the bridge and took the con. I was too busy to be scared, and I assisted as best I could. A few miles into the maneuver, six Japanese tugboats nudged alongside of the carrier and started guiding us toward the pier. The tugs gathered around as close as they could, then the Captain started shouting orders to park the ship. He did it just like parking a Cadillac in New York City.

Exhausted, I went to my stateroom to get ready to leave the ship for some sightseeing, known as "going on liberty." I loved Tokyo and the surrounding countryside, and in those days you could get a Kobe beefsteak for a decent price (nowadays the cost is astronomical). Kobe beef is where they feed the cow beer and hand massage it until slaughter time. You can cut the meat with your fork! It was absolutely wonderful. Deciding to take a ride on the bullet train, I was so disoriented in the foreign city that I couldn't figure out where I was. I was standing on the street corner when a young lady saw me and recognized that I was perplexed and confused. She spoke perfect English and asked if I needed help. I asked her where the train station was and she pointed me down the street. She very politely told me that the station names were in English so it wouldn't be a problem. Thanking her, I made my way through the throngs of people. I arrived at the station and, sure enough, there the name of the station was in English letters, spelling out the Japanese name-no help at all. Riding the train was exhilarating. It was the fastest land trip of my life. The next few days in the city were exciting: the clubs and the restaurants were unbelievable. Crawling back to the ship when the partying was over, my body was still reeling from fun. The next morning we were at sea again and back to our grinding schedule.

Not too long after this trip into Tokyo, I was at the air terminal in Da Nang, Vietnam. We were flying a SH-3A, a highly reliable twin turbine helicopter capable of staying airborne for five hours (not to mention landing on top of water). This is what the President of the United States flies in today. Some yahoo came up with the idea of refueling from destroyers, giving pilots the capability of staying airborne for 10 hours at a time. The concept was wonderful except for a few horrifying details. All you had to do was hover over the end of the destroyer while your crewman hoisted up the fuel line and topped the helicopter off with highly volatile aviation gasoline. If the destroyer was bobbing around like a cork in the rough sea, it was difficult to keep a steady hover and not crash into the ship's masts, antennas or the bridge. The trick was trying to do this at night with very little visual reference and flying mostly on instruments. After you completed this near impossible task, you were strapped in and flew an additional 5 hours, for a total of 10 hours in the air, while sitting in the world's most uncomfortable seat. Fortunately, this dangerous practice was abandoned after many mishaps and problems caused by fatigue.

The helicopter we flew was officially a Sikorsky SH-3A. Max speed was right around 120 knots, unless you were getting shot at, in which case you could usually milk a few more knots out of the machine. We usually had a four-man crew that consisted of two crewmen, a pilot and a copilot. We didn't have hard mounts with weapons, but the two crewmen manned the doors with M-60 machine guns and the copilot hung out of the window with an M-79 grenade launcher. The SH-3A helicopter was originally built for anti-submarine warfare, but it was about to be used in combat for search and rescue.

Hong Kong was a long way off, not only in miles but also in days, as it had somehow dropped off the schedule. We normally never had to stay at sea longer than 30 days, but this particular stint at sea went on and on. The ship stayed off the coast of Vietnam for 90 days without a port call. The only thing that kept some of us sane was the fact that we were allowed to go inland occasionally. The Admiral and a few of his staff would go in and play golf, and, you guessed it, they had to be flown in by helo. This gave us a chance, among other things, to replenish our booze supply-something we needed pretty badly. But there we stood, day after day, on the deck of our ship, looking out on the Vietnamese mainland, not able to comprehend the magnitude of what we, or the republic of the United States, were about to embark upon.

CHAPTER TWO

It was not too long after we had arrived off the coast of Vietnam that the U.S. entered the war. U.S. aircraft were making daily strikes into North Vietnam, and we were doing search and rescue for the guys flying into Indian country. Our mission was to follow the fixed winged aircraft onto the beach as they put in their strikes. If they had problems, or were shot up, we would insert into enemy territory and attempt to rescue them. Not only did we get to see the coast, but also the lights of Haiphong and Hanoi first hand and close up. These cities were certainly well within the enemy lines. We didn't just see enemy territory; we landed on it. We seemed to be in the thick of the battle nearly every day. All of the things that we were promised wouldn't happen to us came to pass; we landed on enemy soil, got shot at, and were repeatedly put in harm's way.

Two months into our cruise, there were twelve aircraft carriers off the coast. Half the U.S. Navy and the Air Force were there, and the war still had no name. One day I was flying a number of logistic flights and landed on all of the carriers that were floating around in the South China Sea. While waiting to land on one of the carriers that day, I saw an A-1 sky raider, a single reciprocating engine, fixed wing aircraft, come back from a strike, all shot up. The aircraft was unable to extend its landing gear, so the ship would not allow it to land on deck. Hearing the ship's air boss instruct the pilot to bail out and a helo would pick him up, I watched the pilot bail out but I didn't see the chute open and I watched in horror as he plummeted into the sea like a rock. His body was never recovered. Later on

I found out that it was a buddy of mine that I had gone through flight training with in 1955.

The Marines, who were stationed on our carrier, were scheduled to make their first strike and we were ordered to fly rescue (RESCAP) for them. It was several months into the cruise and they were itching to get into the battle. The strike was planned deep into North Vietnam. At 4:00 a.m. we had five helos turned up to get on station before the Marines made their strike. The first two helos went up and then it was my turn. The automatic stabilization equipment, engaged just prior to lift off, malfunctioned, the rotors jumped, and the stick flew back into my lap. The stray voltage caused wild gyrating of the helo and uncontrollable movement of the controls. Before I realized it, the main rotor had cut the tail off. Shrapnel and pieces of aircraft flew everywhere. There was a small explosion and other loud grinding and scraping sounds as the helo disappeared around us. I quickly shut the aircraft down. We were left sitting in the seat with the helo still chained to the deck. No one was seriously hurt, but the helo was destroyed, with literally nothing left except the seats and the stick. Looking down, I saw blood running down my right leg and making a permanent mark on the deck of the Yorktown. The flying debris had made Swiss cheese out of three of the Marine A-4 jet fighters parked alongside the carrier island, which were all fully armed and ready for the strike into North Vietnam. Needless to say, the Marines didn't talk to us for a long time after the accident. We never really did find out what caused the malfunction, and I just chalked it up to another hairy night in a long litany of many.

Early the next morning, I was strapped into a new bird (that is to say, a different old bird). Even though they were not straight from the manufacturer, I knew that our helos were in excellent condition, because I was still the squadron's Maintenance Officer for the approximate 16 aircraft. But after the events of the previous night, even I was having my doubts. I was scheduled to fly search and rescue on another night strike. Perhaps I wouldn't have been so nervous if we had been able to fight the war in the daylight hours. So there I was, more than a little unnerved as I sat waiting to take off. The tie-down chains were pulled and I was given the go ahead. Clutching the collective with my left hand and the cyclic with my right I pulled us into the thin, black air. Air is thinner at night, and therefore doesn't have as much lift. Aviators know this, which is why they take extra precautions when flying between dusk and dawn. The nights in Vietnam were getting longer and cooler, making the flight conditions harder and harder to deal with.

We flew until we saw the lights of beautiful downtown Haiphong. The fighter jets and A-1's passed over us and we could see them getting set up for the strike. We watched the explosions bursting in the air as the bombers made run after run over their targets. We held off, waiting to see if we would be called in. Watching the ensuing attack, I could not describe the disconnected feeling I had. Then the call came that one of the jets had been hit and was on its way back. We heard the "mayday" and saw the pilot eject. Spotting him, we realized that he was extremely close to the middle of the city. The inner part of Haiphong was no safer than the surrounding forests and suburbs, since the enemy was everywhere. We followed the pilot's chute as he descended to the ground, disappearing into the thick canopy of trees. About that time we noticed tiny, glowing spheres coming up toward us from the jungle floor. I remember thinking they looked like green basketballs, an impression that stayed with me throughout the war. These were actually tracers from a 50-caliber machine gun. Tracers are nothing more than phosphorus tips on every fifth bullet, causing that round to glow once it is fired. This makes it much easier to zero in on a target, because you can actually see where your bullets are going, particularly at night.

My copilot started popping M-79 grenades out his window. The loud thud they made as they hit the ground was indicative of the firepower we had at our disposal. Yellow smoke was visible in a faraway clearing. We assumed it was the downed pilot activating a signal flare, so we headed for the site. We found out later that sometimes the Viet Cong lit off smokes in a different area than where the downed pilot was, in order to confuse the rescue party. The incoming artillery was getting close. No one could figure out why we weren't getting hit. Maybe we had been hit, I thought, but just didn't know the difference. We hovered over the pilot and a crewman had to go down to help him into the sling. The tracers were still coming at us. Luckily, the sun was finally starting to show. At this point, I wasn't sure whether any of us were ever going to see another sunrise or sunset. We managed to get the pilot, who was covered with blood, into the helo and get out of the Viet Cong-infested jungle. We flew back to the ship and no one said a word. To say that we were in shock wouldn't do justice to what we were feeling. The empty detachment I had felt while observing the war from afar had turned into a sickening awareness of the presence of death, since we were now in the middle of the action. Little did I realize that this incident planted the initial seed of my Post-Traumatic Stress Disorder.

We all went back to the ready room and debriefed the flight. We obviously hadn't made any mistakes, since we not only walked away,, but also saved the pilot. The skipper congratulated us on a job well done, though he told us we probably would not get any medals since the U.S. wasn't officially in Vietnam. We visited the rescued pilot in sickbay; he was beat up pretty badly but was alive. He had lacerations all over his body caused by falling through the jungle canopy. We might not get any medals for this mission, but it was a custom that a rescued pilot would give a bottle of booze to the rescue crew. One of the pilots I rescued said he would leave several bottles of booze for me and the crew in Da Nang. Low and behold, a few months later I stopped into the White Elephant, the Officers' Club at Da Nang Air Base, and there was a gift waiting for us: a couple of bottles of Tanquaray gin.

We went up on the hangar deck to inspect the helo. The air above deck was calm and the sun shone like no other day I had seen. There were a number of holes in the fuselage, near the fuel tank, through the tail rotor blades and in the transmission. We decided from that point on to put our flack vests in front of us on the Plexiglas window between our legs instead of wearing them. Our seats were made of armor plate, which protected the body, but our heads protruded above the edge of the seat, so they were exposed to incoming fire. We also had sliding panes at our side, which we could pull out to cover the sides of our bodies.

We had immersed ourselves in the beautiful Vietnamese countryside for months on our search and rescue missions, and now it was finally time to leave our stations and visit Hong Kong.

Hong Kong is one jewelry and clothing store after another. There are exquisite tailors everywhere where you can have any kind of clothing you want made. Of course, there are also hundreds of restaurants, nightclubs, and bars—all wonderful. Needless to say, it was going to be party time for us in the big city. We had been at sea for so long we had moss growing on us, and we desperately needed to feel like human beings again. We met up with a bunch of Australians who worked in the city. From our bit of recreation with them I learned that you couldn't out-drink Aussies.

The first morning after we partied, I got up and crawled down to the swimming pool so I could hang my sorry head in the cool water. As I was lying there, I noticed a sign that read "massage." I dragged what I could of my body into the massage room. A Chinese man ordered me to get undressed and go into the sauna. After 20 minutes in there, I exited the room, dripping sweat from every pore. The man again ordered me back into the steam room for another 20 minutes. The heat and perspiration were unbearable, and I thought I was going to die. After this, I lay down, and the Chinese man dried me off and placed a bowl of ice-cold orange slices on my chest. After I ate the oranges, the man put a plastic tent over my head, turned on 100% oxygen, and proceeded to give me a massage. It was wonderful. I began to be revived and felt like I might live. When he finished, I got up, tipped him handsomely, and walked out with head held high and sober as a judge. I felt so good that I went down to the bar and drank with the Aussies once again with renewed vigor.

After a wonderful week in Hong Kong, eating in the finest restaurants, getting decent nights' sleep and lots of hot water showers, we returned to the ship for another round of war. Even though the war still had no name, the casualties were mounting, and there were so many troops, ships and warplanes, you couldn't count them. Everyone seemed to be thinking to himself, "This is getting old." We went another sixty days on the line at sea, and finally our 9 months were up and we got to go home.

There were no medals awarded during that time frame, so we didn't get an Air Medal for that tour, let alone a Distinguished Flying Cross, a Silver Star or a Bronze Star. The operations we had been involved in definitely deserved a medal, maybe even a Big Blue (the prestigious medal of honor). It really didn't matter to me, since I had at least returned in one piece. But it would have been nice to receive some recognition for the difficult and hazardous flights we made every day. We certainly didn't get laurels or recognition from the American people. When we returned, anti-war demonstrations were in full swing and Jane Fonda was doing her treasonous thing. Even movie stars were protesting and burning draft cards. College students like future president Bill Clinton were the most vocal objectors to what was happening in Vietnam. There was truly very little support from our countrymen and women.

Once back in the States, I tried to forget Vietnam and not let the nightmares I was having bother me. I received orders to go to Guam and was glad to go to a quiet little island with no war. No problem, I thought. Vietnam was involving more casualties, and, now, prisoners of war. I didn't have to be near any of that. The Viet Cong can't get me in Guam, was how I reasoned it. My assignment on the island was to fly an H-34 Sikorsky single-reciprocating engine helicopter for search and rescue, and a C-54 (DC-4), a four-engine transport, for taking servicemen and their families off the island for R&R (affectionately known as I&I—intoxication and intercourse). During the two years I was stationed in Guam, I made 14 trips to Hong Kong, 10 trips to Taiwan, and 28 trips to Japan, not to mention brief stops in the

Philippines, Okinawa, Bangkok, New Guinea, and many of the Micronesian Islands.

At the end of those two years, the war in Vietnam was still going strong. The Navy was short on logistic aircraft, so they sent me on numerous temporary assignments to Saigon. One of these trips was a three week stint as a logistics flight. The first time this happened, I could not believe that I was in Vietnam again. I knew that I was by the stench of the place when I got off the airplane. Saigon is a filthy city, for it is the only place I know of where rats run in the streets in the middle of the day. You can walk around for an hour, take a handkerchief, and wipe black soot off your forehead. I guess the million diesel motor scooters have killed the air. It was difficult to breathe and the streets were strewn with litter from one end to the other. We stayed in some fleabag hotel right in the heart of downtown. The first three weeks we were there, we flew 144 hours cruising up and down the coast. My job was to fly from Saigon to Da Nang making several stops along the way. Those of note were Na Trang, Phan Rang, and Cam Rahn Bay. I had the crew take out the left bank of seats so we could carry both supplies and passengers. Normally we could carry 70 passengers with all the seats in place, but with half the seats gone we could carry supplies plus 70 Vietnamese who were small and didn't weigh much.

Cam Rahn Bay had a nice long runway. The U.S. had poured millions into the place, and today the Communists are in possession of a huge airbase and deep-water port designed for the 21st century. The rest of the stretch of coast was made up of pristine white sand beaches. I understand now that it's a big resort with numerous luxury hotels. At Na Trang there was an Officers' Club at the end of the runway. We would buy several cases of beer and ice them down all day so we could have a cold one after a long, tiring day. When we landed back in Saigon, it took us about 30 or 40 minutes to taxi to the dust bowl at the other end of Ton Su Nut airport where we parked the aircraft. As we taxied to the parking spot in the sweltering heat, we popped open a beer and enjoyed the cool adult beverage. The flights were relatively uneventful, but very fatiguing, because sometimes there were only a few miles between landings. We had no air conditioning and the cockpit temperature ran about 125 degrees. In addition, we were loaded down so much that it was difficult to get airborne on some of the short runways on hot, no-wind days.

While landing at Chu Lai one day, someone yelled out that we had taken a hit. We touched down and discovered that one of the passengers had been shot in the rear when a round came through the fuselage. Our days were usually 12 hours long, hot, dusty, monotonous, and punctuated with a few moments of stark terror like this one.

One time, we received a tip that one of our Vietnamese passengers, an elderly woman, had explosives on her. We checked and found 50 lbs of dynamite strapped to her body, hidden under the maternity dress she was wearing. God knows how this tiny Viet Cong lady could carry 50 lbs of dynamite on her body. A chill went up and down my spine, for we never knew who the enemy was at any time. From then on, we took extraordinary precautions in searching the passengers. Until then, we hadn't been all that strict with security. I would have felt better had I been on a ship, any ship, instead of this God-forsaken place. At least there, we almost knew who the enemy was.

One morning, we were working on the aircraft before the flight, when a Viet Cong came over the fence and started shooting at us. In an act of bravery, I emptied my .45 revolver at him and ran the other way. The perimeter security guard captured him and put us all at ease. It is one thing when you are in the air getting shot at, but when you are on the ground and almost face to face with the enemy, that's another story. I said a small prayer and hoped that my tour would be coming to a close so I would never have to come back to Vietnam again.

After one of our three-week stays in Saigon, we were all exhausted and ready to get back to Guam. We lined up for take off on the runway at Ton Son Nut. There was a little bit of wind, we had no cargo, and only the flight crew was on board. Earlier in the day, one of our Vietnamese passengers had broken a bottle of Nuc Mam in the airplane. This is a wine-like concoction made of fermented fish and rice and is used as a sauce for cooking. I guarantee that you have never smelled anything like it in your life. With the heat, it made several of us sick. How anyone could use such a vile substance was beyond my comprehension. Wherever that plane is today, it probably still smells of Nuc Mam-the most disgusting smell I have ever encountered in my life. Sometimes other similar scents give me flashbacks and the vile odor returns to my senses, causing my stomach to roll over.

As we headed down the runway, it became apparent that the number one engine was not going to make it. The engine gages were making all sorts of strange gyrations. I was trying to get to flying speed and get the aircraft airborne. The crew looked at me, wondering what my decision would be, whether we'd abort or try to get in the air. If we aborted, God knows how long we would be stuck in Nam. We were light, having no passengers or cargo and only enough fuel to fly to the Philippines. We attained flying speed rather quickly. Jerking the aircraft into the air, I told the co-pilot to raise the gear and feather number one. It was my decision to fly it out on the three remaining engines regardless of the consequences. It was either that or crash on the runway. The crew let out a cheer, they all patted me on the back, and we headed toward the Philippines on three engines. When we got there, we had to replace the bad engine, but at least we were out of Nam and resting quietly in the Philippine islands. It was party time for a few days while we waited for the engine to be replaced.

On one trip I made to Guam from Hong Kong in a DC-4, there was an Admiral's aide aboard. He used to go on trips with us and often brought his wife along. He was a black shoe, a non-aviator shipboard type. He always gave me a ration of shit about my flight pay, which was about $165 per month at the time. We were on our way back from 7 wonderful days in Hong Kong. Flying back to Guam from Hong Kong, I always stopped at the Philippines to refuel before making the 8-hour trip home (that was stretching the abilities of the DC-4). This particular night we were flying on the backside of a typhoon. The trip, which normally took eight hours from the Philippines to Guam, took only six. The tail winds were horrendous. The weather was despicable and we were buffeting up and down-up 2,000 feet, down 2,000 feet. I was white knuckled and had a death grip on the yoke to keep the aircraft right side up. Needless to say, I was scared and I thought we were going to plummet into the ocean and die, in which case I would be responsible. Everybody on the plane was sick except me, because I was too busy flying the plane. After wrestling with the aircraft for 5 five hours, we finally broke out into the clear and the moon and stars were shining brightly. Saying a long prayer, I breathed a sigh of relief and patted myself on the back for what was in my estimation a magnificent job of flying. The stench in the plane was abominable and almost did me in, but I was so happy to be alive that all I could do was smile. When I went to the back of the plane to relieve myself, I passed the Admiral's aide and his wife, who were leaning over and still puking in their barf bags. Laughing out loud, I said, "Hey Al, do you have any more smart-ass comments to make about flight pay?" He looked up with his green face, and in a barely audible voice he replied, "No sirrrr."

On another one of my trips to Hong Kong, I met two men who owned emerald and opal mines in Colombia and Mexico. We started up a conversation and I told them that I had bought some black opals in Australia and was having them set in Hong Kong. They invited me back to their room to view some of the precious stones they had. They were absolutely spectacular. There were thousands and thousands of carats of opals and emeralds. I was green with envy at the sight of the emeralds and wished that I'd had the money to buy a bunch. The two men asked me if I ever flew into Japan, and I told them I averaged two trips a month to Tokyo. They told me that the yellow opals only brought three dollars per carat in Hong Kong but 10 dollars per carat in Japan. They asked me if I would take 150,000 carats into Japan for a fee of a dollar per carat. They said to think it over and let them know the next day. I went back to my room and tried to sleep, but every time I multiplied one dollar times 150,000, it came out the same. I stayed awake all night and thought about this new smuggling adventure I was so close to getting mixed up in. "What would I do with $150,000?" Invest; buy a house or a hell of a car. Maybe these guys would let me make more than one trip.

As the sun came up, I had my answer. The next morning I met with the gentlemen for another sumptuous breakfast and told them pretty much straight out that I couldn't do it and that I was sorry. As it turns out, on my very next trip I had to go to Bangkok and Japan. When I left Thailand, I bought a huge pineapple for 25 cents. When the trip was over, I got off the plane and the customs agent who was there to inspect the plane asked us what our purchases were. He saw the pineapple and asked me where I bought it. I said, "Bangkok." The customs agent said, "Eat it." I did, and almost got sick, even though it was sweet, warm and delicious. As I sucked down the pulp and juices, I could see myself as a convicted smuggler behind bars in Leavenworth for bringing a bagful of yellow opals into the country.

Shortly after that incident, I was assigned to fly the Secret Service in a helo over President Johnson's motorcade. The President was on Guam to meet with a number of world leaders. Prior to the President's visit, the ship repair facility on Guam built a massive table for the conference. It was made out of Filipino mahogany and literally weighed a ton. The only error the carpenters made was that they forgot to measure the size of the doors that the table had to go through. To solve the problem, the table was cut into sections and had to be reassembled in the room. After some dead time waiting for the presidential parade to start, we lifted off with three Secret Service men on board my H-34 reciprocating engine helo. My job was to keep the helo directly over the President's limo by flying in tight circles over the car. The only problem was that there were 40 knots of wind blowing out of the south. It was difficult just staying near the Presidential motorcade, never mind trying to stay right over him. The Secret Service people were screaming at me to get over the top of the car, which had been flown in from the States a few days before. It was a magnificent long black limo with bulletproof windows. Finally, I hovered into the wind at 200 feet, which is a very dangerous position to be in. If we lost an engine we would be well within the dead man's curve and would surely be killed. Flying like this made me nervous as a cat, but I did my job and the Secret Service finally stopped yelling at me.

On another occasion, I was asked by my superior officers to fly General Jimmy Stewart around the island of Guam on a sightseeing tour. At that time, the movie star was serving in the Air Force as a general and an aircraft commander in B-52's. That's when the massive bombing raids that took place over Vietnam began. This beautiful Sunday, I was asked to take the General for a helo flight around the island. Even though I was familiar with him as a celebrity, I didn't dare call him Jimmy. My military training would not allow that. He wasn't very talkative, wouldn't wear a helmet, and just sat there quietly. In order to communicate with him I had to scream over the loud noise of the engine. As we passed a beautiful beach on the northern coast called Tarogi beach, I asked the General, "What do you think of the beach?" His muffled response was, "Ah, Ah nice beach," as only Jimmie Stewart could say it. We finished up the day, and I flew the General to the Air Force base where I made one of my most perfect landings. The General jumped out and thanked me for the trip, and his aide came up and gave me some autographed pictures. The news media descended on me and asked me what Jimmy Stewart had to say about the flight. I told them he said: "Tarogi beach is nice" end of quote. The next day, the newspaper headlines in the local Agana (the capital) newspaper read, "Jimmy Stewart says Tarogi Beach is the most beautiful beach in the world." What I learned that day was that maybe one should take some things in the press with a grain of salt.

All in all, Guam was a successful tour. I rescued or picked up over 200 bodies, both alive and dead, most of which had gotten caught out past the reefs. The beaches truly were beautiful, with crystal white sand and palm trees swaying in the breeze. They were also very dangerous, with vicious sharks and notorious rip tides. Portions of the island had magnificent cliffs as well. The island was only 7 miles wide and 37 miles long, but it somehow managed to contain seven golf courses and 6 military bases. Now, Guam is a favorite destination for Japanese brides and grooms. It is a gambling Mecca with numerous resorts and casinos.

As soon as I left this Pacific paradise and returned to the States, I received orders to Pensacola, Florida. My assignment was to be a helicopter flight instructor, and, in many respects this assignment was very rewarding. Since the war was still going on, my main purpose was to instruct students in the art of helicopter flying so they could go to Vietnam. Each flight that I made with a young new pilot, I thought of the possibility that he might have to go to Nam. This thought was disturbing because of my past experiences, and how I had coped with them when I was in Vietnam. My Post Traumatic Stress Syndrome was progressing, as I had experienced flashbacks of my previous tour. Payback time would come when these fledgling aviators went to Nam, so I became extremely critical of their performance. When I was a flight instructor the first time, I wasn't as critical as I was after going to Vietnam. When I joined the Navy right after Korea, I never dreamed that I would have to go to war. Now that I was training pilots to fly in combat, it was a different story. My conscience would bother me if I didn't train these aviators the best way I knew how.

While sitting in the ready room in Pensacola in the summer of 1969 waiting for the weather to clear (in the instructing environment, you usually don't have to fly in inclement weather, so we sat around and watched "Victory at Sea" movies), the phone rang. I didn't know the call was for me, but the ring had an ominous shrill sound. It turned out to be the man in Washington who detailed people to new military assignments. I knew that I was due for a nice cushy job in Norway or Bermuda and had just been selected for Commander. I wasn't worried about my next assignment. The detailer said he had a good offer for me in Vietnam, and it would be good for my career. I told him that I had amassed a number of flight hours under adverse conditions in combat, and that I didn't need to go back. I also reminded him that I had already been awarded an Air Medal for my service on temporary duty from Guam to Vietnam. Expanding on the matter, I told him that I had already served two tours in Nam and that I would just about go anywhere in the world but there. He explained that they were establishing a new command in Da Nang, and the Admiral wanted a slick pilot, which meant someone who would fly a UH-1L aircraft without guns. (These flights were to be logistics runs only with no combat, but all the rules had changed in Vietnam.) The detailer then made it clear that I had no choice, since I had just been selected for Commander, had previous experience in Nam, and most importantly because the Admiral had specifically asked for me to be the Officer in Charge (OIC) of the detachment. The detailer again assured me it would be good for my career. I realized that I had no choice and tried to negotiate the agreement by specifically requesting to be sent to gunship school at Fort Rucker, Georgia (just incase things went haywire, and they did). He said the Admiral wanted me right away and any additional temporary duty would be out of the question. So, in November of 1969, I had my best friend fly me to New Orleans from Pensacola to catch a plane overseas and serve my third tour in Vietnam.

CHAPTER THREE

About this time, my nightmares started again. All I could think of was facing incoming machine gun and mortar fire again. This assignment was supposed to be semi plush with almost no combat, but I was smart enough to know that was just not going to be the case. I had a sick feeling in my stomach that my life would be in danger every single day of my new tour. The fact that I might encounter the possibility of killing somebody in combat didn't help either.

I was on my way to Nam and flying halfway around the world for the second time in my life. The only good thing I could find about the trip was that I didn't have to travel via boat. White-knuckled all the way to Saigon, I just couldn't believe I was on my way back to Nam for the third time. I landed in the capital city, and the stench in the air overwhelmed me and brought back vivid memories of the two previous tours. A squadron helo picked me up and took me to headquarters in Binh Thuy, which is south of Saigon. The skipper greeted me with the news that the Da Nang detachment was not a go and had been scrapped. Since I had not been to gunship school I would be a slick pilot and remain at the palace guard in Binh Thuy for my tour of 365 days. Rage and anger came over me at this twist in my life, and shortly after I began counting the days again. I struck the days off of my calendar, as if I were a prisoner of war behind enemy lines.

The squadron I had been assigned to was the Helicopter Attack Light Squadron Three (HAL-3). Lt. JG. Kevin Delaney (later to become the Admiral Delaney who wrote the forward to this book), who was supposed to go with me to Da Nang, was selected as my co-pilot. It just so happened that the Commanding Officer of HAL-3 was going on R&R, for what we were told would be an extended period of time. Lt. JG. Delaney and I wrangled an assignment flying slicks in the jungle for a couple of weeks for the first duty of our new tour. An old friend of mine, Commander Ken Hamman, was the Officer in Charge of the detachment at Ben Luc, on the Co Dong River. We headed almost immediately to his base so he could give me a short course in gunship driving. It was my only chance to get out of the slick assignment and have some opportunity to help win this war.

Ken taught me what I needed to know about weapons, ammunitions, explosives, and killing; still, there I was, flying slicks with very little excitement. I knew that the longer I was there, the more anxious I would get for some action, and anxiety is what causes a fighter to make mistakes. I either needed to get into battle or find some way into a leadership position–one that would allow me to make decisions instead of waiting for others to make them for me.

As chance would have it, one of the Officers in Charge was wounded by enemy fire, and the squadron was short of qualified people to run a detachment. The skipper was in a bind and had no choice but to assign me to be the Officer in Charge at Nam Can, otherwise known as "Sea Float," a series of eight barges tied together in a large river. Sea Float was also the southern-most outpost in Vietnam territory, and because of its vicinity to the U Minh forest and detachment, one saw plenty of action.

It was January 1970 when I arrived at Sea Float, and there were over 150 people living on the barges. Tents were constructed on the upper surface of the barges and there were two helo pads on one end. The pads, constituting a very small area, were not lit, so we had to do some tricky maneuvering at night in order to get the helos down safely. The barges were about two feet above the water and there was not much visual reference for landing. We shared quarters with a group of Navy SEALs who all looked like the current Governor Ventura of Minnesota. They always appeared rag-tag because they blackened their faces and wore headbands. They also rarely shaved—it made them more invisible if they didn't—and Lord knows they wanted to be invisible against the enemy. They usually had two to four bandoliers of bullets over their shoulders, hand grenades strapped to every thing that would hold one, and enough fire power to end the war that very minute. The Sea Wolves, which is what my squadron was nicknamed, were to support the SEALs in their mission to interdict the jungle area surrounding Sea Float, including the U Minh forest. At the same end of the barge where the helos were parked was all of the ammunition needed to support the operation. In one large pile were thousands of rockets, hundreds of thousands of rounds of ammunition, and crates of M-79 grenades.

When the helos needed gas, we had to go on shore to refueling stations that were scattered throughout the Delta. If we went to a Navy-run refueling station, or Petroleum Oil and Lubrication (POL), as they were called, it took ten minutes just to fill out the paperwork. If the Army ran it, we simply gassed up and flew away. The Army apparently never had anybody sign for anything-a policy we liked immensely. As a result, we hardly ever went to the Navy POL's. Between strikes we could usually take a leak, fill up with fuel, and load ammo and rockets-all within three minutes! Army pilots would drop in and get out of their helo while it was still running, refuel it, climb back in, and fly off into combat. The Navy would never stand for any of these wild, unsafe practices, but the Army didn't seem to mind and I never saw a mishap with this modus operandi. The first time we did a quick ammo/fuel stop, several young Vietnamese kids jumped out of the jungle and starting helping the door gunners load rockets and ammo. They were exceptionally knowledgeable about weapons systems. I was petrified at first, because we had no way of knowing if they were Viet Cong or not. I was eventually reassured by my experienced door gunners that this was a normal thing, and that we were relatively safe. We just had to be alert and watch them like hawks. It took some getting used to, but it certainly did speed up the arming procedure and got us back into combat quickly.

The Viet Cong made it a personal project to try and destroy the barges at Sea Float. They would send divers with 100 pounds of TNT down the river on many nights. The enemy used hollow bamboo shoots to breathe below the surface of the water. We were wise enough to post guards at either end of the barge that would drop concussion grenades every 20 minutes to deter the Viet Cong from doing this. In the morning we would find at least one dead Viet Cong washed up on the bank of the river. It actually didn't take us long to get used to grenades going off all night. The explosions had an eerie sound as they echoed off the steel bottom of the barge. It sounded like submarine sonar echoes bouncing off a ship. It is one of the many sounds of war that I will never forget.

The water surrounding the barges at Sea Float had all sorts of creatures running through it. There were sea snakes in the river and rats that would run all over the barges looking for scraps of food. There were so many rats we couldn't give them all names. When we weren't fighting, we sometimes got together with the SEALs to talk about the last go round in the jungle. There we would be, drinking and carrying on, when one of the SEALs would yell, "Skivvy check!" Everyone would pull down their pants, and the guy who had skivvies on got thrown in the river. I had no real need to meet the sea snakes, so I never wore skivvies (a habit I took to civilian life but eventually had to discard). Every once in a while one of the new guys would wear skivvies and away he went, right over the side; he would never wear skivvies again, maybe in his lifetime.

One evening the SEALs were in a world of shit. We scrambled to cover them and transport reinforcements from their team into the hot zone. After we had inserted the SEALs, I took off as fast as possible in order to supply them with friendly fire. We were taking fire from every side when, all of a sudden, we heard a loud explosion. I realized right away that it was our helo, and before we knew what was happening, we began to lose altitude.

My mind flashed back to October 1967 when I was stationed in Pensacola. One of our assignments there was to instruct astronauts in flying helos. The astronauts were taught to fly helos because the Lunar Excursion Module flew in a very similar way. The command personally assigned me as the flight instructor for two NASA astronauts, two of the best, in fact: Harrison (Jack) H. Schmitt, and Owen Garriott of Skylab II. Jack was assigned to Apollo 17 and was one of the last men to walk on the moon. They assigned him to me since we spelled our last name the same and the Navy thought it would be good press. Owen Garriott was later assigned to Skylab II. Both men were civilian astronauts with Ph.D.'s in Geology. Jack had received his degree from the University of Oslo in Norway. Both men had less than 450 hours total flight time, which actually turned out to be a plus, because they didn't have to unlearn all of the bad habits that fixed wing pilots tend to acquire. Habits I had learned myself. When I transitioned to helos in 1963, I had 3500 logged hours in fixed wing aircraft. It was incomprehensible to me that when you make a descending left turn in a helo, you have to use right rudder because of the tail rotor torque action.

The aircraft we used to train the astronauts were TH-13M Bell helicopters and TH-57 Jet Rangers. These guys jumped in and flew the helo for the first time like they were born in it. It was an honor and a pleasure to teach these wonder pilots.

One of the maneuvers we taught the astronauts was full auto rotation. That is, we shut off the engine, dropped the collective to maintain the inertia of the main rotor blades, flew down with no engines to about 50 feet, pulled back on the stick to slow the forward airspeed, lowered the nose (which put us at about 25 feet), and slowly pulled up on the collective to slow the main rotor blades down and cushion the landing. The idea was to land softly with no forward speed, very little rotor RPM and zero airspeed. If you pull up on the collective when you are too high, you run out of main rotor RPM and crash. Though it is a dangerous technique, even in training situations, we repeated it over and over until the astronauts got it right.

Years later, Jack invited me to Houston. I took him up on the offer and made the cross-country trip to see him in Texas. When we met up, Jack gave me a number one tour of the NASA complex. Seeing all the equipment and computers, technicians and scientists was an amazing sight. I remember saying to myself that I was proud to be an American. We had been so successful in the Apollo missions, and, for that matter, in all the other missions, that I felt genuinely lucky to be a part of the United States Space Program.

That same night Jack invited me to his condo for a party with some NASA people. "This is going to be an unbelievable experience," I thought to myself, and it was. After just receiving my BA after 16 years of night school and six different universities, I was wearing the biggest graduation ring I could purchase. It was my badge of honor for my perseverance. There were about 50 people at the party when I arrived-all astronauts, scientists, engineers, meteorologists, geologists, and physicists-an incredible assortment of minds. There were more Ph.D.'s in the room, it seemed, than there were in the entire world. Sitting next to one of the astronauts, I made some small talk, and told him I had just graduated. He asked me what my Ph.D. was in. I was embarrassed and couldn't even answer. I just mumbled under my breath that I had just received a Bachelors degree.

Everyone was talking about going to the moon and what they would do when they got there and how they would handle the moon rocks. Finally, someone told a joke that made everyone laugh, and I didn't get it. Someone else told a joke and the same thing happened, I didn't get it. Then I got up the courage to tell a joke, and no one laughed. I was mortified and realized that I was in way over my head. Someone passed a Playboy magazine around pointing out a comic with no caption that pictured peacocks with their feathers in arrays of structure. Those who saw it died laughing and I was again humiliated and didn't get it. I closed the magazine and told Jack thanks for a very nice party and slipped out the back. I was so depressed I almost threw my graduation ring in the garbage.

The date was December 6, 1972. There were three

thousand invited guests sitting in. There were three thousand invited guests sitting in bleachers on a pitch-black night when Jack Schmitt, along with Eugene Cernan and Ronald Evans were on their way to the moon on Apollo 17. We had enjoyed a sumptuous dinner and a tour of the exhibits at the Space Center. Then, we were brought in buses to the launch pad. We literally had front row center seats, as close as one would care to be. The launch was scheduled for 9:53 p.m. The countdown started and my heart surged in my throat. As the countdown proceeded, they realized there was a problem. Mission control stopped the countdown and my heart left my throat. Finally at about 1:00 a.m. the countdown began again. I should have been tired, but it was so exhilarating to be there, knowing that I had contributed to such an incredible moment in our history. Everyone knew this would be the last trip to the moon for a long time, though no one ever guessed why a halt was put on the program. The mission for Apollo 17, the sixth lunar landing mission, was to explore the Tarus-Littrow area of the moon. Finally after an interminable wait the countdown went on: "10-9-8-7-6-5-4-3-2-1- We have ignition!" Mission control was as calm as Frank Sinatra on a Vegas stage. The Saturn rocket lifted ever so slightly, and then a few feet more. The 3,000 people in the bleachers and many thousands more at home watching on TV gasped as the rocket hovered. Mission control gave the word: "We have lift off." After what seemed like another million minutes, the rocket lit up the sky, gained momentum, and began its momentous journey to the moon. While Jack was on the moon, he named a crater -- the Schmitt Crater. I couldn't believe it! Jack had named a crater on the moon after himself and me be association. We had a crater on the moon named after our families -- the Schmitt Crater.

The successful space mission lasted 12½ days and splashed down at 2:24 p.m. EST, December 19, 1972, about 500 miles southwest of Samoa in the Pacific Ocean. The recovery ship was the USS Ticonderoga with an SH-3A helicopter, which I had flown previously. Shortly after the successful mission Jack and the crew of Apollo 17 toured the country. When they came to

San Diego, where I was living at the time, the press held a news conference. Unfortunately I was not aware of it and did not get to be there. However, when I turned on the 6 o'clock news that evening and heard Jack say, "Thank you, Art, for helping me make this mission successful." Goosebumps rose all over my body, and I was elated at the thought of my contribution. Being only one person away from landing on the moon, I have been extremely fortunate to be associated with this spectacular and historical event.

The explosion brought me back to reality, and I realized we were hit and were about to crash. I realized that I had no power and was headed straight for the ground. We were hit, but only God knew by what, and from where it came. I knew that I had to do a real time, full auto rotation in a severely damaged helo with no power, and land it as safely as I could, with no damage to the aircraft and no injuries to the crew. It took every bit of skill I had learned from doing full auto rotations with the astronauts to land the helo safely. Fighting for control of the aircraft, I got us close enough to the ground to make a soft landing. However, when we hit, our helo rolled up into a ball. The controls had been damaged; the aircraft was almost uncontrollable. Fortunately, we all scampered out of the wreck in reasonably decent shape. Later, I learned that this crash did irreparable damage to my back. My wingman swooshed in and we unloaded his ammo, saved two rockets, and all climbed on board and flew away from the wreckage. It was a bitch getting into the air with the extra weight on board, but we made it, after a long run to pick up translational lift. My wingman shot the two rockets into the wrecked helo on the ground, and it exploded in a great burst of flames. We always did this so the Viet Cong could not get the leftover guns and the ammo. We were told shortly after we got back that we had been shot down by a ten year old kid who was hiding in the weeds with a claymore mine. The SEALs killed him, and that is how we found out he was so young.

After eleven months in Nam, it was finally time to go on

R&R, but in this case it was going to be I & I. One of my young fighters and I had the opportunity to travel and party together in Hong Kong. It was either that or go to Australia. Since I had so many wonderful experiences in Hong Kong, it was time to return and participate in the good life that I had enjoyed my previous trips. We boarded an Air Vietnam 737 in Saigon. I had a little trepidation since over the past 11 months I had learned never to trust a VN of any type, and now I was going to let one transport me in a commercial jet. That's the kind of attitude one develops while living in constant fear, and we certainly were afraid of any Vietnamese in any shape or form. Whether it was fear that a sapper would lob a grenade into our hooch or set off C4 explosives under our ship, we experienced the emotion constantly in our daily dealings with these people. It even started making me have irrational thoughts and constant fear of not knowing who the enemy was. Nonetheless, I decided there on the runway to take a chance and trust the Vietnamese commercial pilots. Looking out the window on to the tarmac, I realized the window had a crack in it. I said, what the hell. There's no difference between dying here on the way to Hong Kong or getting killed in action on Vietnamese soil.

We took off, and the stewardesses offered us a sandwich and a warm beer. (In those days flight attendants were still called stews, a term that has since been struck from the vocabulary of the American people.) It was a short trip to Hong Kong with bumpy weather, but I didn't care much. We approached the airfield, and I remembered how much trouble it was to fly into, because the end of the runway stopped right at the base of the skyscrapers in the heart of downtown Hong Kong. I prayed that the weather would be decent. If there wasn't at least a 1500-foot ceiling and three miles visibility, we would have to fly back to Vietnam. My prayers were answered when the Vietnamese pilot slammed the plane into the ground on the end of the runway and we screeched to a halt at the other end. I gazed up gratefully at the skyscrapers above us in beautiful downtown Hong Kong and was ready for party time.

We hustled off of the airplane and had the usual hassles

with customs. I didn't bring many clothes because I planned to get a whole new wardrobe custom-made. We took a cab to our hotel, and I could almost feel the clean sheets and the hot shower against my war-torn body. Getting to the room, I poured a stiff Martini, got into the tub, and lay there for an hour or longer. The hot clean water was a sensation that was truly better than sex. We didn't realize how deprived we were back in Nam, and, shaving with hot water for the first time in 6 months, I thought I had died and gone to heaven.

I met my young friend downstairs, and we proceeded to walk the streets in awe of all the goods in every store window. It was like Christmas in July. Every visit to Hong Kong was wonderful. The city is so vibrant and full of nightlife and shop-till-you-drop opportunities. There were no bad restaurants and just rows and rows of jewelry shops and clothing stores in an extremely clean town. Hong Kong is truly a magnificent city; I could move there tomorrow without even thinking about it. We stood on the street corner and gazed up at one enormous office building after another, all lit up in green and blue neon lights. We passed by a men's store and there was a gorgeous young blonde standing in the window with a tie, motioning to us. We went in and found out she wanted our opinion on a tie she was buying for her father. Of course we were experts because for the past 15 years we had been wearing black ties with our uniforms, so we advised her. In reality, we had not even seen a tie in over a year. Nevertheless, she selected a tie with our help. We wisely invited her for a drink at a nearby English pub. It turned out that she was once Miss Scotland and now worked as a flight attendant for an international airline. Miss Scotland was 5ft. 8in. or so, built like a brick shithouse, and dressed accordingly. My young warrior pilot disappeared into the night with her, and I didn't see him for the duration of the trip.

The rest of the week I shopped, drank, and bathed. I was invited to the British Embassy for a party and was mingling with fellow officers when a waitress came around with some hors d'oeuvres. I ate one of the treats, which were absolutely delicious, so I devoured about a dozen of the little things.

When I asked someone what they were, I was told that they were fried grasshoppers. My appetite left me shortly after that, though they were certainly better than the "lurprats" we ate in Nam (lurprats are long-range patrol rations). All you do is add hot water and voila! spaghetti or ham and eggs. They are edible but packed with thousands of calories, so if you make a steady diet out of them, you will weigh a ton and never be able to get airborne.

The next day we were scheduled to go back, but rumor had it there was a typhoon brewing. Being of sound mind and body and a commander in the U.S. Navy, I thought it might be prudent for me to remain in Hong Kong until the typhoon passed. I decided to go to the airport the next morning anyway and check the weather again. I was considering the possibility of two or three more days in Hong Kong (with the excuse of a typhoon). The only catch was that we'd probably be sent to the brig upon our return for being AWOL (absent without leave), not to mention facing court martial time for not coming back on time. Thus, I chose to go back to the stinking war. Miss Scotland and my warrior buddy eventually showed up. There were stars and tears in their eyes. It was a sad moment, and I revisited my decision to go back or remain in Hong Kong. Looking at the lovers and the Air Vietnam airliner, I once again I concluded that discretion was the better part of valor. They kissed in a long embrace and parted, never to see each other again.

Dragging my wounded friend on the airplane just as it was getting prepared for take off, I curiously and enthusiastically asked him what had happened all week. He said it was the most fantastic sex he had ever experienced in his life. Of course, any comparisons at this point were completely academic. He said she kissed and sucked every part of his anatomy, and he gratefully reciprocated. "Well what else did you do?" I asked. He hesitated for a moment while thinking of the question. "We showered together," was his response. See, I told you, a shower is as good as sex. He said they ate a few meals and did a little sightseeing. He bought a tie for his father and a pair of socks for himself. I said, "Is that all you did? What did you do the rest of the time?" He said they just screwed and made love all day and night. He said it was the first time his thumb has come repeatedly. I related the story of the Embassy party and my many purchases made during a small shopping spree. My friend laughed and then cried over his loss. Before going to Hong Kong, I used to take my wings from my uniform and bend them around my finger into a ring. However, there wasn't much gold in it and my finger always turned green. While in Hong Kong, I went to an old jeweler who made two rings for me. One was a pinky ring with a tiny pair of Navy wings on it, and the other was a reproduction of my flight wings fashioned out of 14-carat gold. They each cost 20 dollars and were beautifully made.

Hong Kong was a great time and I was almost rejuvenated enough to go back and fight. I had only one month left to my tour, and now that I had lived it up for one week, I was scared to death that I would not live to see its end, and perhaps never again experience the pleasures of the material world.

We were sitting around waiting to be scrambled when one of my flying buddies told me a story about a trip he had made to Hong Kong. He was in a restaurant one night when he saw a very attractive woman at the end of the bar who was dressed very well in a fitted suit and carrying a handbag and gloves. She was elegant in her stature and he could smell her subtle perfume all the way from the other end of the bar. He approached her and started a casual conversation. They had a couple of drinks and she told him that she lived in Resolution Bay, an upper class community of high-rise condominiums. She asked him if he would like to go back to her place for a drink. My buddy thought, "This must be my lucky day." He had been on the ship for several months and was more than horny.

They went back to her condo, which was long, narrow and elegant, just like her gorgeous body. There was a bar at the end of the living room with a huge picture window behind it. The window had a magnificent view of the city, with all of the sparkling lights and tall buildings. She really smelled good now, as he was standing next to this woman with a magnificent figure.

She unbuttoned her suit coat and her blouse was open down to her navel. Her supple breasts were more than he could handle. They were large and perfectly shaped with huge nipples. She lit a cigarette and told him she was going to get into something more comfortable. He practically ejaculated on the spot. She poured him a drink, left the room, and appeared a few minutes later in a sheer white negligee. Her body was a fantasy that no man could resist. You could see everything she had, and her skin glistened under the gown. Her hair was ablaze in blonde. She came toward him and slipped her tongue down his throat until he thought it hit his navel from the inside. She opened her gown and everything in its perfect shape was there for him to visually swallow up. She grabbed the lump in his pants and dragged him to the front of the apartment. He was so excited that he could not handle the thought of lying on top of her. To have this magnificent woman and all of her beauty would be more that he could have ever prayed for. She opened the door to her bedroom, and there was a man laying in the bed nude, smoking a cigar and reading a magazine. He looked at my friend and smiled. He shuttered at the scene, which conjured up all sorts of horrible thoughts. The woman, whose name was Lilly, said, "You can have all of me, every way you want and for as long as you want, just as soon as my husband gets through with you." He looked at them both in disbelief. He could not conceive of the situation he was involved in. He felt shocked, confused and sick. He was no longer aware of the woman's elegant beauty, and he turned away, saying, "Thanks, but no thanks," as he bolted for the door. He couldn't sleep for two nights, and never went back to that English pub. In fact, it was a long time before he could bring himself to talk with a woman in a bar. I told my buddy that I didn't believe his shocking story. He immediately pulled out a white lace handkerchief and let me smell it. After I touched the small souvenir, there was no doubt in my mind that that woman existed and that the incident did indeed occur.

CHAPTER FOUR

The skipper of one of the Landing Signal Tank (LST) ships invited us all out to his boat one day for a home-cooked meal. It worked out that one of our helos was operationally down, so we were able to take him up on his offer. When we got out to the ship in the afternoon, we all took advantage of the facilities, including the warm showers. When we were all cleaned up, we proceeded to the dining room (unfortunately once again in our soiled flight suits) where there was an elaborate turkey dinner waiting for us. The skipper of the ship greeted us as we all stood at attention around the wardroom dining table. He explained that the little brass bell on the table was the puck, and whoever the puck was in front of would be served first and must say grace. One of our men who we had nicknamed "The Animal" was standing in front of the puck. He looked down and said, "Oh shit, I have the damn puck." I turned three shades of red, but the skipper understood that the Sea Wolves were all animals, so we sat down for dinner. The Animal said a warm, meaningful grace. The food was wonderful with turkey and all the trimmings and ice cream, and we didn't even have to add water to the plastic bag. We were able to spend the night there, and that meant clean sheets. The skipper offered me the Admiral's stateroom on the ship. It was a nice sized room. We always traveled with a little booze, just in case we had a lull in the battle. Many years after that, I ran into the skipper, and he admitted that he knew we drank on the ship. Though there were strict rules against having alcohol aboard a Navy vessel, he said he knew we needed a break and if he had thrown us all in the brig, who would win the war?

After our mini-vacation, we were back in the field, and if it hadn't been for the helicopters, we could have sworn we were in Hawaii. I was always awestruck at how beautiful the countryside was in Vietnam. Sunsets were particularly beautiful as the light glistened off the water, and there was water everywhere. In fact, there were basically very few roads. The only way to get around was by sampan in the rivers and canals or by helo. When I was on the ground, I would listen to the sound that helos made as they flew. The rapid chopping sound the blades made as they cut through the air did much to disturb the tranquility of Vietnam. No wonder we got shot down; you could hear our helos coming from miles away.

It wasn't long before we were called in on a nasty mission. The SEALs were in another sticky situation and taking fire from many directions. In minutes, we were flying down the river in a torrential rainstorm. (The weather was generally pretty good in Vietnam, usually hot and dry, but when it rained it really came down, especially in the monsoon season.) It was just after dusk, but, fortunately, there were enough lightning strikes so that we could feel our way up the river between the trees on the banks. When we arrived at our destination, we immediately started dropping parachute flares, our way of simulating daytime and giving us a clearer view of the field. There were several things that could shed light on nighttime firefights: flares, lightning, night-seeing scopes and binoculars, even a full moon. All these things made it easier to see the enemy, but it also made it easier for the enemy to see us. The parachute flares were very effective, but when the illumination wore off you were back in the black night and it took a few minutes for your eyes to get readjusted. Even so, we continued to fire off flares, and they lit up the entire night sky.

Something about the situation reminded me of my twenty-first birthday. I was flying P2V's at the time, a four-engine (two reciprocating, two jet engines) aircraft. (The P2V is the predecessor to the P3V Orion that recently made an emergency landing in China.) We were on antisubmarine patrol, 100 miles out from Argentia in a torrential rainstorm with lightning and severe turbulence. All of a sudden, there was a loud crack as a bolt of lightning went past my right shoulder and through the back of the aircraft. Needless to say, I was stunned and shocked, and I quickly called to the crew to see if everyone was all right. They were fine, but the lightning had broken the glass nose dome, which normally would have had an aerographer sitting in it if we were on ice patrol. The tail cone was shattered, and there were several small fires in the aircraft that the crew fought to put out. The instrument panel was in shambles, all of the radios were gone but one, but we were still flyable. We called in a mayday and started looking for the nearest field to make an emergency landing. After we landed, I asked the crew, "If this was my twenty-first birthday, what is the rest of my life going to be like?"

I'd had many close calls with stormy weather. In August 1969, when hurricane Camille hit the Biloxi and Gulfport Mississippi, I was called up from Pensacola to help evacuate survivors and the injured. Several of my men and I arrived after the hurricane had hit, but the wind and the rain were still fierce. We must have had 60 or so helos milling about in and out of the rain and the clouds. We were flying H-34's, Sikorsky reciprocating engine helos capable of carrying 10 or so people. We also had Bell Jet Rangers, TH-57's, that held 4 passengers (if we stuffed them in). We also had some UH-1 Hueys capable of carrying 5 or so. Our task was to evacuate 10,000 people to an area as far north as we could, preferably somewhere in Northern Mississippi. As I let down from 1500 feet, I could smell the stench of death and sewage. The smell became overpowering, but we were too busy maneuvering between helos, buildings, power lines, and people to give it a second thought. A few of us managed to land in the parking lots of grocery stores and other unlikely places. People would jam into the helo on top of each other. The crew chief would try to keep the crowd down to ten. Even though the wind was very strong, it actually helped the helos fly. We sometimes took too many people on and we could not get into the air. We would then have to ask one or two passengers to get out and wait for the next ride. It was pandemonium. On one of my lift-offs, I flew over a mobile home park that was completely demolished and flattened. I had thought at one point of setting my parents up in a mobile home. I changed my mind right then and there.

I had been sent on a similar hurricane operation when I was assigned to VP-8, an antisubmarine squadron in Norfolk, Virginia. I was a young aircraft commander, a lieutenant junior grade who was flying a multi-million dollar aircraft. I was the designated Hurricane Evacuation Officer. It was my duty, when a hurricane was identified and heading our way, to fly to the Air Force Base in Chanute, Illinois. My responsibility was to ensure that billeting was available for the pilots and crew. When a hurricane got within 12 hours of hitting the base, the squadron would fly the remaining 11 airplanes to Chanute. My job was to fly to Chanute several days prior to the squadron's arrival when a storm was on its way toward our home base. The Captain was trying to get a record month for flight time, but the hurricane was upsetting the apple cart. Making the decision to take my Ensign co-pilot on a touch and go training flight was a bad decision. On the second landing, the Ensign had the nose too low and the nose gear hit the ground first. This causes the aircraft to porpoise and bounce between the nose gear and the main landing gear. The options are to try and abort the landing and attempt a semi-controlled crash (while also converting it to a semi-controlled landing), or attempt a wave-off where one gets off the ground for another pass. Both maneuvers are equally dangerous, but I elected to attempt a landing.

Things starting breaking off after the third bounce, beginning with the nose gear and doors for the nose gear. The propellers started hitting the ground and spraying shrapnel everywhere. Then the two jet engines hit the ground and began breaking into pieces. I looked out my window and saw a fire truck following us down the runway. I finally got the plane stopped, and about that time we burst into flames. We all evacuated the aircraft from the rear hatch, which was about 12 feet in the air, and the fire was put out almost immediately. We were taken by ambulance to the hospital to see if we were

all okay. We were, so we went to the Club for a stiff drink. I
called the squadron leader and told them I had a problem and
needed a few parts: a nose wheel door, nose gear, two 3450
reciprocating engines and two J-34 jet engines. In other words,
just about everything but the body.

When I flew back commercially to Norfolk, the skipper
had a big chunk of my ass. I asked him if I could fly the plane
back when it was repaired, since I was responsible for the
wreck. Big mistake. 3 weeks later I did fly up to test the aircraft,
and soon after that we proceeded back to Norfolk. Sure enough,
we got caught in a horrendous thunderstorm. There I was, at
18,000 feet, bouncing around with four brand new engines. I
thought for sure I was going to die that night and be punished
for my bad deeds.

The rain pounding on the helicopter brought me back to
the reality of trying to stay alive and finish our rescue mission.
My wingman screamed at me, "Sea Wolf One Six, it looks like
they are shooting something bigger than 50-caliber at you!" It
could have been hand-held rockets, radar guided missiles or
whatever, but it was getting hot. Seeing the green basketballs
coming up at us from the machine guns scared the shit out of
me. We were attempting to put in our strikes in the midst of
all the havoc. We were firing rockets, all 14 of them, and the
50-caliber and 60 caliber machine guns were blasting out the
door. The detachment had a five-foot tall Chief Petty Officer
who was bouncing up and down as he shot a gun that was too
big for the little guy to handle, but he was a magnificent shot.
He could hit a gnat off of a Viet Cong's ass and wipe out a whole
village in one fell swoop. The co-pilot was shooting the grenade
launcher out of his window and I was blasting away with the
mini gun. We had not perfected flying low and cutting a swath
with our swords. My peripheral vision caught the fuel gauge,
which was dropping rapidly. We had apparently taken a 50-cal.
bullet or more in our fuel tank. Obviously, we didn't get hit with
one of the tracer bullets or we would have been blown out of

the sky. The Crew Chief immediately started dropping more parachute flares to light the way for a fast, controlled crash. I spotted a small clearing and dove for it, and as I pulled up on the collective, I killed the RPM of the rotor blades, which resulted in a soft landing.

We were under fire from the Viet Cong in the weeds. The SEALs and my wingman were covering us. There was so much firepower that the sky was lit up without the flares and there were explosions all over the place on the ground. My wingman found an even smaller clearing than we had, and swooped in to pick us up. We shut down our helo and ran like hell for the other aircraft. We jettisoned everything we could so that we could get airborne in the thin air. My wingman jerked the controls of the helo, putting us right in the midst of green basketballs. Why we didn't get hit then, or why we didn't blow up when the bullet hit our fuel tank, I will never know. We flew back to base and said a little prayer for another night without any serious injuries. In the midst of the confusion and havoc we made the error of not destroying the helo. When we went back the next day the Viet Cong had completely stripped it. All the ammo, doors, windows, tail rotor and main rotor blades were missing.

Every day was the same thing: we would load the ammunition up in the evening and ready the helo for a scramble. Depending on the wind and the heat, we would carefully load the helo because it could become nearly impossible to lift off if we loaded the craft to the hilt. We carried 14 rockets with anti-personnel war heads (2,000 metal darts which would disperse over the heads of the enemy), an M-60 machine gun, an M-79 grenade launcher, 7.62 ammo for the mini gun (which fired 4,000 rounds a minute), and our own 45 or 38 caliber handguns (depending on each man's personal preference). We also carried a couple of 50 caliber machine guns just to make sure we could defend ourselves.

One day, I was flying with a new Ensign as a copilot. I had actually flown with him when he was a student in Pensacola. I explained to him that when you are fully loaded and it is a hot, no-wind day, you have to be particularly careful on take off because it takes a long time to gain translational lift. If the buzzer, which indicates a low RPM, starts screaming and the light starts flashing, the crewmen must immediately jettison the rockets and throw the ammo out the door to lighten the load. It is imperative that the pilot doesn't pull up the collective in his left hand to try and get airborne. If the pilot pulls up on the collective, the main rotor blade pitch increases, the RPM drops off dramatically, and he will crash the aircraft. The helo was definitely fully loaded and it was a very hot, no wind day. We were taking off from the barge, which was only a foot off the water. As I started the take off run, we were only a few feet into the air and directly over the water when the low RPM warning light came on and the buzzer began banging in my ears. I wanted so much to pull up on the collective and try to get in the air. I probably would have if I hadn't just given the lecture about hot, no-wind days to the Ensign. The crewmen were on the ball as usual. They immediately jettisoned the rockets and threw all of the ammo out the door. I kept my arm stiff to prevent me from pulling up on the collective. We were only inches from the water, which was slick with no wind, even though our rotor wash was pushing down and aft. Slowly, after we had gotten lighter, the airspeed began to increase and the RPMs picked up. The helo started to gain translational lift and ever so slowly became airborne.

The Sea Wolf skipper decided he wanted to fly a night mission with me. So I went out to the ship, took a wonderfully long shower, and climbed back into my smelly flight suit. The skipper and I prepared for the mission. We would depart from the LST, which barely held 2 helos. The main rotors were within a foot of each other when we turned up to fly. That particular night the Commanding Officer of the ship was experimenting with deck lighting. The ship really had no deck lighting, like a carrier, had on board. The Commanding Officer had rigged life vest flashlights intermittently along the sides of a rope ladder down the side of the ship. It was like a string of lights down a runway. At any rate, it was a piece of cake flying off the ship. It was 60 feet in the air, compared to the Sea Float barge, which was only a foot and-a-half off the water.

Recalling my first night carrier landing, which was executed while practicing sub hunting off the coast of San Diego, I was reminded just how different it was here in Nam. It was in California that I learned the answer to the question, how do you get from 150 feet and 60 knots to a 40 foot hover and zero airspeed at night? The answer: you do it on instruments, and you do it very carefully and meticulously. Anyway, that particular evening the weather took a turn for the worse, and the ceiling and visibility quickly went to zero, zero (zero feet visibility, zero feet ceiling). Since one of our missions was to support the antisubmarine warfare effort for the fleet, it made sense to someone to keep the helos out until they were down to five minutes of fuel. There were two of us flying around in this miserable, sticky soup. The ship talked us around the carrier controlled approach pattern (CCA) to a final approach. The weather was truly awful. We made one pass and never saw the ship in the dark night and poor visibility. We were critically low on fuel, and the low fuel warning lights were glaring at us like demon eyes in the night sky. On the second pass, the ship talked us down to 150 feet and a quarter-mile behind the ship. At that time, we engaged our automatic equipment, which flew us down to a 40-foot hover. We saw the wake of the ship and disengaged the automatic stabilization equipment. We flew up the wake until we could look up and see the flight deck lights, pulling straight up and landing. On touchdown one of my engines flamed out because of fuel starvation. My heart was in my throat, my hands were sweaty, and my knees would have been knocking except for the cyclic stick between my legs. The pilot of the other aircraft, who was a Naval Academy graduate and had a bright career ahead of him, promptly unstrapped himself, went down to the ready room, threw his wings at the skipper and said, "I quit," and walked out. I hoped there would be no more night carrier landings like that one, but, of course, there would be. Not being smart enough to turn in my wings, like the Energizer Bunny, I just kept trucking along. It was hard to believe that the air boss and squadron leader would put us in such a dangerous position in such shitty weather.

The skipper and I were scheduled to cover the SEALs in a night insertion into the U Minh forest. We were ready for take off; it was last light, pitch black, and no moon. Moonlit nights are wonderful and beautiful, except when you are flying night-shooting missions. Helo gunships make wonderful targets in the moonlight. We pulled up on the collective to increase the pitch of our rotor blades so we could become airborne. We were off and on our way into the thin black night. My wingman lifted off behind me, and I heard a loud bang and my helo shuttered, coughed and grunted. A bright red light on the console lit up and blinked repeatedly, "hydraulic failure". The helo instantly became as hard to fly as a buffalo with wings. I had to literally muscle every control that made a helo fly to keep it in the air. Glancing over at the skipper, I could see that he looked a little green. It was as black as it could get outside. Screaming, "Mayday! Mayday!" into the mike, I'm sure I sounded pretty frantic as I contemplated how this event might turn out. My options were to fly over water some 20 miles to our land base, land on one of the closer unlit barges, or land back at the ship. The ship was a few miles behind me. Even though the deck was small, and I would have to make a run on landing in a very limited space, it seemed like the right thing to do. One thing that Naval Aviators are taught to do is make correct life threatening decisions at a moment's notice. I muscled the helo around, looked out into the thin, black night air, and there was the ship, all lit up like a Christmas tree. Thank God the skipper had decided to leave the lights on while trying to get them set up just right. The other reason it made sense to land back on the ship was the fire fighting equipment on board. Flying the helo with no hydraulics was one of the most difficult emergencies I have ever had to deal with in my career. My copilot, the skipper, asked what he could do to help. I told him to hold on tight because I didn't know how hard we would hit. The crew just sat quietly and watched, since there was nothing they could do but sit there in the pucker position. They had already jettisoned the ammo and the rockets, and this meant we would have no fun on the SEAL raid that night. This emergency landing was my cookie, and no one else could do it. Approaching the ship I started to let down as smoothly as I could. My arms weighed a ton and were getting tired as I muscled the controls of the helo. Reducing the power, I came over the edge, pulled up on the collective, touched the skids down, and rolled a short way across the deck. It had to be a short run, because the deck was small and the ship's island holding the Commanding Officer was right in front of me. It was a rough landing, but, as we used to say, any landing that you walk away from is a good one. We stopped and shut the helo down. The skipper reached over and shook my hand and said, "Well done." I unstrapped, went back to my stateroom, and had a stiff drink. The secret stash of liquor we had was precisely for nights like this.

We played the board game Risk for two days, on and off, until someone came with parts and the crew fixed the bird. Fortunately, I was senior to the Commanding Officer of the ship so I could occupy the Admiral's stateroom, since there was no Admiral on board. One night we locked the door, had a few drinks and watched "Paint Your Wagon" four times.

Reflecting back to a similar hydraulic emergency that I had had a few years back when I was flying off the Yorktown, reminded me that I was either a skilled or a lucky pilot. When the Yorktown visited Sasebo, Japan, we would fly the birds across the mountains to Osaka to a Japanese maintenance facility. I was the Maintenance Officer, so I assigned myself the nice job of making the trip. Osaka was great liberty and the Japanese did a marvelous job on the aircraft. After three wonderful days in Osaka, going to the Kabuki Theater and getting a hotsi bath (like a Jacuzzi) and a massage, we flew out of Osaka to Sasebo. Halfway across the mountains, we smelled the pungent odor of hydraulic fluid. The crew checked and found about an inch of fluid in the bilges. About that time, the hydraulic failure warning light came on. We were too far across the mountains to turn back, so I continued on to the Yorktown. Immediately, I shut down the radios and as much of the electrical equipment that I dared to. The crew sopped up whatever fluid they could from the cabin floor. When we about 30 miles out, I turned the radios on and called the ship and declared an emergency. We alerted them to get the fire crew on the flight deck with their equipment. It was unbelievable that we were in such a pickle, particularly after we had just come out of a maintenance check. Flying over the last mountaintop, I could see that there was no one on the flight deck manning the fire equipment of the bridge. I had no choice but to fly the turkey into the ground or, in this case, the deck of the ship. I pulled the helo into a hover and lowered the gear manually. About that time, a crewman appeared and gave me the signal that he was going to insert the pins to keep the landing gear from collapsing on touch down. After landing safely, I discovered that a hydraulic line had become uncoupled. Little did I know that I would have to do a similar trick under wartime conditions on a ship much smaller than the Yorktown.

The bird was finally fixed and we flew back to the beach. That night, word got around that the base was going to be overrun by Viet Cong. Needless to say, we were all on alert. Fortunately, the skipper was still on board and wanted to get into the thick of things. Around dusk, incoming mortar shells began exploding randomly all over the base. We launched into the moonlit night. You can't always pick the nights you want to fight. Right after takeoff we started taking fire from all directions. The green basketballs began again from the Viet Cong's 50 caliber machine guns. The skipper, who had been in a lot of combat, said he had never seen anything like this before. We found where the mortars were coming from and started laying in strikes. There was a little wind, and we were very close to the battle, so we could load up with almost all the ammo and armament we wanted because of the proximity of the helo pad and of the battle. We put in about six strikes and fended off the Viet Cong in an intense and effective battle. The next day, we went down to the base for breakfast, which we normally never did. We weren't welcome because we were the "cast off" aviators with smelly flight suits, so we never went down to the mess hall. This day, however, there were people practically laying palm fronds at our feet as we walked through the compound. The base now understood what the Sea Wolves were all about and knew how effective we could be in a firefight. Most said they had no idea what kind of firepower we had at our disposal and what kind of damage we could do to the Viet Cong. We never got much crap from the base people or the Base Commander after this awesome display of power. Prior to the previous night, they all thought we were fooling around when we went out to fight.

Occasionally, we would reload and refuel from the LST's that were stationed very close to the shore. They were sometimes closer to us than our home base or other refueling stops. On one particular day, we had put in several strikes in a village close to the shore. It was a spectacular show for the guys on the ship. One boat had an ordinance man who was particularly efficient and who hustled all the time. It was beyond me how this overweight Petty Officer could move so fast. Sitting in the helo as we were refueled, I asked the skipper of the ship if I could take the ordinance man with us on the next strike. He gave his consent, and we left one of our gunners behind as we strapped in the ordinance man and hit the strike zone. In between unloading the rockets, I was firing the mini-gun 4,000 rounds a minute, the door gunners were shooting the 50 and 60 caliber machine guns, and the copilot was shooting grenades from the grenade launcher out of the window. We were picking up heavy fire from the village. I glanced behind me at our passenger, who was white as a bed sheet. He clearly couldn't believe what we did for a living. You could tell he had no idea what went on every time he and his crew loaded our helo to fight. We took a couple of hits in the fuselage and finished the strike. We went back to the LST, reloaded, refueled, checked the damage, and dropped off our passenger. He was still pale, but he admitted that he had had the time of his life, and was thrilled with the opportunity to participate first hand in a real battle. Believe it or not, every time we came back to his ship, the ordinance man hustled twice as fast as he had in the past.

As the Officer in Charge of a detachment of helos, with 12 officers and 12 enlisted men, I split the crews in half so that we were on duty 24 hours and off duty 24. Even though we were off duty, it didn't mean we weren't working, it simply meant we didn't have to fly that day. The days we didn't fly we stacked ammo, filled sandbags, and cleaned weapons. We readied the helos in the evening, fueling and loading them. If we were scrambled, the off duty crew started the helos; the on duty crew jumped into their flight suits and boots, put on their weapons, and jumped into the helo. We could be in the air and shooting within 2 minutes of the phone ringing, even out of a dead sleep. Sometimes we did this 3 or 4 times a night. There were nights when I rolled over and asked myself, "Have I been flying tonight or not?" I still have nightmares about these missions. Today, if the phone rings at night, I jump out of bed and am a nervous wreck for hours afterwards. After that, I can never get back to sleep because so much adrenaline has poured through my system. I complain to my step-daughter, who has the habit of calling us after 9:00 p.m., that she has no idea of the magnitude of what a late phone call does to my psyche. This is just another Post-Traumatic Stress Syndrome symptom that has emerged from my stressful time in Vietnam.

The helos we flew were UH-1 B's that were loaned to us from the Army. Needless to say, they were in sad shape, and were practically held together with bailing wire and chewing gum. We never went on a mission in the UH-1's unless we had two of them up, so that they could fly cover for one another. One night, one of our birds was down because of a mechanical problem, and this put us out of commission until the problem was solved and the aircraft was fixed. This rule came into play one evening when the SEALs scrambled us because they were in deep shit and needed some air cover quickly. We declined the mission because we didn't have two operating birds, and we never flew with just one. My Maintenance Officer, a young Lieutenant, said that he was willing to fly the bird in the downed condition. I told him, "Absolutely not!" I didn't want to endanger him or the crew. My troops didn't think this was the right decision because the SEALs were in trouble, but I stood my ground and my guys wouldn't talk to me for days. However, I was the boss and I had to look after my men. Another detachment took the mission and the SEALs were rescued. But I took a lot of heat because of my decision not to go on the mission.

With the hectic flying schedule we had, plus all of the fighting going on all the time, it was a miracle that we didn't go crazy. We were so young that we didn't know what stress was; we all coped with it in different ways. At night I used to lie in the tent listening to tapes of Dionne Warwick singing Burt Bacharach's songs, becoming emotional, and crying. "Do You Know the Way to San Jose," "The Windows of the World," "That's What Friends Are For," "Alfie," "I'll Never Fall in Love," "Promises, Promises," and "Don't Make Me Over" were some of the songs I listened to. I get very worked up when I listen to Dionne Warwick even now. She deserves a medal of honor for getting me through the war. Just recently, I bought tapes of her old hits and am desensitizing myself with a mild regimen of exposure therapy. I have now been able to listen to the tapes several times without getting too upset.

The subject of the drug problem in Vietnam comes up a lot. Drug use was rampant with a lot of grass smoking going on, but I managed, I think, to keep it down to dull roar in our detachment. There were drugs, but the flight crews were good about generally not using hard drugs. We all worked so hard and we tried to keep occupied in other ways when there was an infrequent lull. All we did was a little speed to get up for the flights and alcohol to crash on the days we didn't fly. The drug and alcohol problem was not so pervasive in Vietnam because of the ravages of war, but rather because of the boredom we so often faced.

Patrol Boat River-Swift Boat

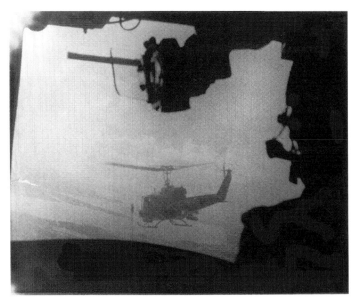

UH-1B on Patrol

Searching Vietnamese fishing boat for weapons

Gunships on patrol with airboat

Rocket attack

UH-1B Gunship

Rocket attack

Gunships on patrol with PBR's

Gunships on YRBM

Cockpit view

Crew arming gunship

Rocket attack from cockpit

Gunships on patrol with PBR's

UH-1B Gunship, rocket run

UH-1B door gunner

UH-1B door gunner

M-60 machine gun in action

7,400 total flight hours, 521 carrier landings, 210 night carrier landings, Bronze Star, 21 Air Medals, Vietamese Air Medal, Combat Action Ribbon, Presidential Unit Citation, Navy Unit Commendation, Mertorious Unit Commendation, National Defense Service Medal, Armed Forces Expeditionary Medal, Vietnam Campaign Ribbon, Vietnam Service Medal, with one Slver Star adn two Bronze Stars, Republic of Vietnam Campaign Medal, Vietnamese Presidential Unit Citation.

Front Row Left to Right: Ted Doolin, Frenchy Bordeau,
Randy Rende, Sam Goodwin, Jim Petrovich, LtJg George, Dan
Locke, Carl, Nelson
Second Row Left to Right: Mike Lagow, Ray Wickstrom, Olby,
Mike Suldo, Rudy Deatle, Art Schmitt, Mike Eltmon,
Scotty Gordon, Mike Mendez, Bob Christianson
Third Row Left to Right: Chief Reyna, Rich Lambert,
Mike Dobson

PBR's
Ready for River Patrol

THE NATIONAL AERONAUTICS
AND SPACE ADMINISTRATION
Cordially Invites
You to Attend an

APOLLO LAUNCH

at the
John F. Kennedy
Space Center
Florida

R.S.V.P.

THE UNITED STATES' SIXTH LUNAR
LANDING MISSION
LIFTOFF: 9:53 P.M. EST, DECEMBER 6, 1972
JOHN F. KENNEDY SPACE CENTER, FLORIDA

Mission Goal: Explore the Taurus-Littrow area of
the Moon

The Crew: Eugene A. Cernan
Mission Commander
Captain, USN

Ronald E. Evans
Command Module Pilot
Commander, USN

Harrison H. (Jack) Schmitt
Lunar Module Pilot
Civilian Scientist-Astronaut

Mission Duration: 12.9 days

Splashdown: 2:24 p.m. EST, December 19, about
500 miles southwest of Samoa in
the Pacific Ocean

Prime Recovery Ship: USS Ticonderoga

Seal Team One
Nam Can

HAL-3
Det One - Flying off of YRBM 20

SH-3A
Refuleling from Destroyer

Binh Thuy Hal-3
Hangar at night

Solid Anchor
Det One - Rec rrom and barracks

Sea float - Detachment One
Nam Can

CHAPTER FIVE

We had heard a rumor that they might build a land base on the shore near Sea Float. I couldn't imagine what it would be like without the concussion grenades going off all night. It was true, construction soon began, and we were told to move ashore. The name of the new base was Solid Anchor, located near the village of Nam Can. There was a lot of Viet Cong activity there, so you can see how far south the enemy had penetrated. The Sea Bees, who were building the base, were under fire all the time. Obviously the Viet Cong didn't want the base to be built. The Sea Wolves would scramble regularly to keep the Viet Cong from making mincemeat out of the base. The base was well under construction when we discovered that its perimeter stopped at the helo pad. It looked like the Sea Wolves were going to camp outside the perimeter.

When the helo pad was completed, we set up our tents and proceeded to fill sand bags for our shelter-5000, to be exact! I counted them. We were all out filling sand bags one hot and dusty day, when my troops reprimanded me: "Commander, you are the boss, you don't have to do this." I said, "The objective is to get this sucker built as fast as we can, so we can have a safe place to go when the Viet Cong come over the wall." The base was eventually finished, and the commander was nice enough to set up perimeter patrols as well as a sentry post near us inside the compound. This afforded us some protection. The base commander put two outhouses outside of the perimeter for inhabitants on the end of the base close to the gate. We had our own privies close to where our hooch's were. Unfortunately, the base privies were on the edge of the helo pad. When we came in for a landing, if we noticed that there was someone in the privies, we would transition to a hover very close to the building so we could pound sand up their ass. In fact, one day we were so close we blew it over, occupant and all. Needless to say, the base commander was pissed. Of course, when the sun went down, the gate was closed, and we were literally in the weeds by ourselves.

In order to survive in Nam you had to barter. The Sea Wolves had the barter system down to a science. We would take toothpaste and cigarettes from the sundry packs sent by the Red Cross and trade with the Vietnamese in the village for crabs. Then, we would fly the crabs to the ship and trade with the Filipino stewards for ice cream, paint and floor tile. After that we would fly the ice cream back and trade with the Sea Bees for wood, tools and nails. That's how we built the hooch we lived in. Fortunately, we had a few guys who were handy with a hammer. We built two structures: one for the pilots and one for the crew. The front half of the pilots' structure was like a huge recreation room, while the back half was where we set up our bunks with the mosquito netting over them, because Vietnam had mosquitoes as big as B-52's. We built a table for the front half to seat 12 people. Now we could play bridge, but only two of us knew how to play, so we taught the rest of the crew the rules and we had a ball. There was always a game of Risk going, and we switched players as each of us had to fly our missions. We built a 22-foot bar in the recreation room, and asked the SEALs to help us finish it and celebrate the new nightclub opening. One talented SEAL took his flamethrower, torched the front and made a beautiful smoked design on the front of the bar. We then varnished it, and it was a magnificent piece of artwork.

Our new home, which we had financed, scrounged, and built ourselves, became a bone of contention with the new base commander. Base commanders were sent from Saigon every 90 days to qualify for their end of tour medals. Very few of them had combat experience and they all made our lives miserable. In his infinite wisdom, the new commander said that we were not authorized to build the structure because it was his base. However, we were outside of the base and he had no jurisdiction. Who was going to stop us anyway, the Pentagon? One day, as I was on the floor of the hooch, laying tile that we had scrounged from the ship, the commander came in and said, "You can't do that." "Why not?" I asked. He said, "It is against policy to change Navy facilities without the permission of the base commander." "First of all," I said, "This building is not on the base, and I am the Commanding Officer of this property. You provide no security and no support for us. Besides, we built the building and we maintain it, and we will damn well do what we want to with it. Get your ass out of here. Beside I am senior to you," Which I was, by one number. The next morning we woke up to a ruckus outside of the hooch. A jeep was unloading a dozen or so body bags and putting them under our hooch. I asked the driver what he was doing, and he said the base commander had told him to deliver them there until the Army Dust Off (medical helo) could pick them up. I told him to leave and dumped the body bags onto *our* jeep. Then I drove them down and put them on the porch of the base commander's office. I screamed at him, "How do you like having the body bags at your place?" The base commander sent a message to my Commanding Officer saying that I was not cooperating with him. The next day the skipper came to visit. It didn't take very long for him to realize that the base commander was a medal-hungry, sucking turkey from Saigon and an absolute asshole.

It was good that the Army was over there. They basically had no accountability for anything. We had heard that an Army group needed an air-conditioner. We scrounged one from somewhere and traded it for a "loach," which is a small Army helo. The Army had a number of these sitting around. It was great having a spare helo for logistics and shopping. Most of the time, we didn't have the time to account for what we needed. We had heard that an above ground pool had been stolen from the Army in Saigon. It was packaged and waiting for shipment somewhere in Vietnam. The pool never showed up anywhere in the Delta. It must have been camouflaged awfully well. The mystery remains.

Occasionally an Admiral would come to visit us from Saigon to see what the war was like. My troops would say, "Let's go trade and see if we can get steaks and lobster for his visit." I said to my troops, "No, let's feed him lurprats like we eat all the time, so he can see what it is really like down here in the jungle. He eats steaks all the time in Saigon."

When I was back at the palace guard, before I went to the detachment, one of my assignments was to put on a Change of Command for the old and the new Commanding Officers of the Sea Wolves. This was another lesson learned in the art of making due. I found the only band in the country and brought them to the base for the Change of Command. Four Admirals were scheduled to attend the festive event. Captain Marty Twite relieved Captain Reynolds Beckworth. I had people stationed at the helo pad with walkie-talkies, who let me know when the dignitaries arrived. I found the only organ in Vietnam and had it brought in to be played for the reception at the Officers' Club. We had champagne, shrimp, crab and several roast beefs. Through some miracle I had also arranged for a USO show. I don't remember who did the show, but I know it sure wasn't Bob Hope! None of the Admirals or the Captains could understand exactly how I pulled this miracle off. It was a flawless and unbelievable event, never to be duplicated in Vietnam. The Admiral asked me about various things, "Where did you get this?" or "How on earth did you find such an item in this God-forsaken country?" Must be my Brooklyn, New York upbringing, I thought. One thing you learn in New York, a city where ten million people live on the same block, is survival. We were certainly in survival mode here in "Indian country," and there were an awful lot of Indians and not many amenities.

Once a month, we went back to the palace guard for an Officers In Charge meeting. Those were always a thrill, for it gave us a day or so to unwind and not have to worry about someone coming over the wall. A friend of mine worked for the CIA, whose local headquarters were in beautiful downtown

Binh Thuy, a few miles from the Sea Wolves' headquarters. My comrade would invite me down occasionally for a beer and a swim. In the middle of the Vietnamese town was this little Shangri-La. It was a compound with 12-foot white stucco walls and tall palm trees around the compound perimeter. In the middle of the compound there was a swimming pool and on all four corners of the compound were towers with guards. We would go there and vegetate any time we had the opportunity. It was like going to another planet or another universe. On one of the trips to the CIA compound, we borrowed the Executive Officer's jeep. When we left to go back to the palace guard, it became apparent that someone had stolen one of the fan belts out of the vehicle. We saw the smoke rising out of the hood, but kept driving the jeep. If we stopped and tried to get repairs, we, and the jeep, would be history. We drove into our home compound and there was the Executive Officer standing there watching us drive hell bent for election into the garage. Needless to say, we never had the privilege of borrowing the Executive Officer's jeep again.

One of the things that never made sense to us was the disparity between our pay and the Air America pilots' pay. They were employees of the CIA. Every time we made a rescue, we got a point toward an Air Medal. When the Air America pilots made a rescue they got ten thousand dollars. Maybe this was just a fantasy that we had heard about, because we all said that if we got out of this we would come back as Air America pilots and get rich. Only one of our pilots came back and flew for Air America. He was killed trying to collect his ten grand.

Whenever it was time again for the Officers In Charge meeting, we all looked forward to swapping war stories. One of the meetings took place over the Fourth of July. That evening, we were eating some Australian lobsters that the skipper scrounged for us, and all hell broke loose. Some jerk started popping parachute flares to celebrate the Fourth of July, and everyone starting shooting. It was a spectacular display, but very unnerving and unnecessary, and it didn't do anything for our disposition. I guess the people at the palace guard didn't get enough action, so they had to do their own little thing. So much for Fourth of July celebrations. To this day, I cannot handle the noisy traditions that accompany the holiday. All of the Officers In Charge had seen enough, and we needed a rest so we all bedded down for the night. Since the last Officers In Charge meeting, an Admiral had put a trailer with a 12-foot fence between the two Bachelor Officer Quarters. We were all partying on the second deck of our building, so it just seemed natural to throw empty beer cans into the Admiral's patio. The next day at our meeting, the skipper walked in and grabbed a beer out of the tub he had provided to us for the meeting. We were all too hung-over to even think of a beer at that hour (i.e., 7:30 a.m.). As he swished down the beer, he began to lecture us about the pros and cons of throwing empty beer cans into the Admiral's compound. He had a look of sarcasm in his eye as he lectured us, but we took the lecture to heart and tried not to throw too many more cans the Admiral's way.

At that meeting, an Officer In Charge told us a story about one of his pilots. The pilot was getting ready for a daylight mission and was putting his flack vest on while standing in front of the helo. Somehow, stray voltage passed through the helo and a rocket fired accidentally. The rocket, which has fins on the rear that extend when fired, shot between the pilot's legs, and the crew scurried to his rescue. It turned out that the only damage was to the fatty tissue on the inner part of his thighs. He was cut up real badly and it was a bloody mess, but he still had the family jewels. It was a miracle that he was standing in such a position that the rocket did only minimal damage. We all thought it might be best if we spent as little time as possible in front of the helo before we mounted it to fly.

The meeting was over and I was getting ready to go back to the detachment. A young Sailor asked me for a lift back to his base, which was on the way to our place. We didn't carry a full load because we were only transiting, so we had room for an extra passenger and his duffel bag. We took off and were on our way, when my crew chief called me over the intercom and said that the Sailor's duffel bag was moving around like there was something alive in it. We ignored it and flew on to our destination. When we landed to drop the Sailor off, I asked him what was in the duffel bag and he said, "Oh that's my pet boa constrictor. Do you want to see it?" I said, "No thanks," and we took off. From that point on we always screened our passengers for the contents of their luggage.

One day we got a call from Saigon, and Admiral Zumwalt wanted to fly over a canal-cutting ceremony. The Army Engineers Corps had built canals between Thuy Non and Tre Cou. This would enable the riverboats to extend their coverage of the jungle. They had constructed the canals to within a few feet of each other. The idea was that they would explode C-4 (plastic explosives) and this would connect the two canals as the water rushed through. It was similar to a ribbon-cutting ceremony. Admiral Zumwalt asked me to fly down near the canals so he could get a closer look at the action. I told him we were close enough. He said, "Let's get down lower." I dropped as close as I dared. The C-4 went off, and bang! the helo was pushed sideways, several feet from the force of the explosion. Mud dripped from all over the aircraft. The Admiral apologized and said he appreciated me getting closer to the canals. We flew back to the base, dropped the Admiral off and washed the helo down. It's tough when you're almost shot down by your own friendly fire. I reminded the Admiral of this adventure when we met again at the Sea Wolf reunion in Jacksonville many years later.

From time to time, we had a Vietnamese woman from the local village clean our hooch. We were too busy to empty the trash and do things like that. The detachment consumed copious quantities of Mateaus Rose' wine, since it was 80 cents a bottle and very attainable. When we finished the wine, we would break the bottles and throw the debris in an empty 50-gallon drum outside of the hooch. We didn't leave the bottles intact because the Viet Cong would make firebombs out of them. One day, I noticed that the drum was getting full with the broken bottles, so I told the woman, whom we called Mama Son, to make sure that it got emptied. She broke into tears and was all shaken up, so I got an interpreter to find out what the problem was. The interpreter told me that Mama Son had tried, but the drum was too heavy. When I tried to move the drum I found it impossible to do so. She was right, there was so much glass in there it weighed a ton. We all laughed, left it there for the duration and preceded to fill some more drums. We never did have a corkscrew to open the wine so we used a Bic pen and a sock. We wrote to the Bic pen company and told them about the Bic pen and the sock, and they sent us a gross of Bic pens-just what we needed! A few years later, I saw a Bic pen commercial on TV, and sure enough they were opening a bottle of wine with a Bic pen and a sock. All we had was the memory of the incident and a few leftover pens—no residual money from the commercial that we had perpetrated.

The powers that be in Saigon urged us to use Vietnamese soldiers on our strikes. The SEALs absolutely refused. But I thought I would follow orders, so I asked a couple of Vietnamese soldiers if they would go in with us on an insertion. We got all loaded up and out of the woods came these two soldiers, one had no shoes on and the other had no weapon. We asked the interpreter to ask them what the deal was. They said they forgot. This is what we had to put up with. They got their stuff and we took off. Fortunately, it was a fairly quiet insertion and we didn't need their help. I never used them again. I sent a message to the palace guard and told them what had happened, that this Mickey Mouse practice of using VN soldiers should be knocked off.

We were out flying one night when the SEALs called and said they were taking heavy casualties. We found the SEALs and the firefight, and we went in with four helos. We were taking fire from every direction when the SEALs popped a flare and I found a spot to land. Not being able to land, I hovered with my skids in the water in a rice patty. The SEALs started loading the wounded on board. We had to drop some ammo to lighten the load—no time to be doing this. We heard several loud explosions and we knew we were in the middle of a mortar attack. Our flight surgeon, Doc Spence, who bore a strong resemblance to Jim Brown, and was a product of the inner city of Chicago, was on board my aircraft performing a tracheotomy. The helo shook with the explosions and the blood was spewing all over the cockpit. My copilot was wiping the instruments clean as I tried to maintain a stable hover. (The one thing I will always remember about the War With No Name is listening to the sounds: the helo's engines, the rotor wash, the sound of mortars going off, and the extremely loud repetition of the M-60 machine gun going off right behind my shoulder.) Doc had his hands full, as we all did. I was too busy to be scared and knew we had been hit several times, but everything was working and we were still in a hover. We were running low on fuel and I didn't know the condition of the wounded on board. I didn't think any of my men were hit so I made the decision to get out of there. Pulling up on the collective, I started leaving the hover when a mortar went off beside us and filled the cockpit with mud and splattered it all over the outside of the aircraft. I didn't know which was worse, the blood or the mud, but I continued to make the takeoff run, and was hoping that we didn't run into a mortar or a tree. My wingman covered us as we lifted off, and we were finally airborne and out of there. We landed and loaded the wounded aboard a jeep. The jeep had sand bags around the sides, and I never have figured out what protection that was when we were taking fire. No such thing as an ambulance, I guess.

We didn't sleep much that night, even though we were exhausted. At first light, we all simultaneously got up and, as if by magic, went to the helo and inspected the damage. It was a mess. There were 125 50-caliber machine gun bullets in the fuselage. The engine cowling had a huge gash in it, and one skid was pointing straight up. There was so much blood and mud inside and out that you couldn't tell if it was a helo or a bulldozer. I turned to my maintenance officer and said, "I think it's down. Why don't you have the guys pull it apart and see if there was anything else that we didn't see." We all looked at each other, and it was not until then that we realized we were all now officially scared. The Doc wanted to know if it was always like that down there. We told him it was, and inquired whether he would care to stay permanently.

Doc Spence was an African American gentleman who had worked his way up to Chief Petty Officer, got out of the Navy, went to medical school and came back to the Navy as a medical officer. He pinned his Gold Oak leaves on as a Lieutenant Commander while he was stationed in Vietnam. Doc Spence and several others and I had a wetting down party when we got promoted. It is a long way from seamen to Lieutenant Commander, a medical degree, and a flight surgeon. It was an incredible accomplishment for the good doctor. He worked tirelessly day and night and tried to single handedly wipe out Venereal Disease in Vietnam. Occasionally, he would come down to the detachment and go out on patrols with us. He was always welcome, but more than that, he was an inspiration to us.

One time, when I was waiting to see the Doc back at the palace guard, I overheard him counseling a young Sailor about safe sex. The Doc had told the Sailor if he had to go into town and have sex, that he must use a rubber and practice safe sex. The young sailor said he did: he put the rubber on and screwed the hooker and then he took the rubber off and turned it around and screwed her again. He couldn't understand why he had developed Venereal Disease.

When his 365 days were up and he was going home, Doc Spence was awarded a Legion of Merit, a Silver Star, a Distinguished Flying Cross, and nine Air Medals. He was the most decorated flight surgeon in the Navy. The doctor they sent from the States to replace Doc Spence lasted two weeks. He asked for a transfer, saying there was no way he could live up to the Doc's accomplishments and reputation. The Doc was truly an amazing person. He was assigned to a residency in radiology at Philadelphia Naval Hospital after his tour in Vietnam. Unfortunately, he was struck and killed by a drunk driver on the streets of Philadelphia after stopping to help a woman with a flat tire. What a tragic ending for a wonderful human being.

It seemed that the flight surgeons we encountered were always incredible people. Though I suppose they would have to have been, since they gave up practicing civilian medicine to risk their lives in the war. We had one top-notch flight surgeon in HS-4 (Helicopter Antisubmarine Squadron Four) aboard the Yorktown in San Diego. He took exceptional care of the pilots and all of their families. One night I was watching the six o'clock news, and they had breaking news that a helo from Imperial Beach (Ream Field, California) had crashed and they had no word as to the extent of the incident. I knew our flight surgeon was flying that night, so I jumped into the car and raced down to the base. Just as I pulled up to the sick bay parking lot, the ambulance arrived. The flight surgeon was being taken into the hospital, and I found out that two crewmen had been lost. They had launched a number of helicopters for search and rescue but nothing could be found. Apparently the helo flew into the water. Helos at night never got above 150 feet and we would fly on instruments down into a hover at 40 feet. It was a very tricky maneuver and done with much skill and cunning. When I spoke to my friend the flight surgeon, he said the only thing that saved him was the training he had received in Pensacola. We were taught that if we were down below in the cabin and the helo went into the water upside down, we were to reach overhead and find the strap that led to the door. In the pitch-black night and sinking in the water, he had found the strap and led himself to safety. We all went back to his house and had a drink. A few days later we flew out to the spot where the crash had taken place and dropped a wreath in the water. The Chaplain had a brief ceremony as we flew over the spot. It was a sad day for our squadron mates.

A similarly sad day occurred when we were at Yankee station off the coast of Vietnam. I had three roommates on the ship, and we lived in the last bunkroom under the port catapult. The noise was horrendous when aircraft were being launched. One night, we were playing bridge in our stateroom while one of our roommates was out flying. The phone rang, and the duty officer shouted into the phone that a bird was down. We all scrambled to the ready room. There was a "mayday" call and then silence. We volunteered to fly search and rescue and flew all night. There were several other helos out, and we had to go through a process of elimination to find out which helo was down. It was the helo with our roommate. We were airborne within a few minutes and had three helos looking for survivors. Finally, at dusk, we found two seats and other debris but no survivors or even bodies. We had lost our roommate to the sea and dark night. After a great number of hours searching, the operation was suspended, as the weather was getting very bad. The wind and the rain had picked up to about 35 or 40 knots. We flew back to the ship and were all saddened once again by the loss of our fourth shipmate. The three remaining roommates had to inventory his gear and ship it back to his wife. Last year, at the Squadron reunion in Charleston, South Carolina, we had a bronze plaque made and had a memorial service aboard the Yorktown for our roomate who was lost at sea. Some 30 years after the accident a memorial was finally in its proper place.

The Sea Wolves were called in to cover a PG (a 100 foot patrol gunboat) going up the Nam Cam River. It was broad daylight and the detachment had two helos covering the boat as it went up the river. All of a sudden, the skipper of the ship yelled, "Incoming!" We could see the tracers and the mortars hitting all around the boat. The skipper of the PG was hit and wounded. The Sea Wolves rolled in and put several strikes in the area where the fire was coming from. We suppressed the fire and the PG sailed on down the river to safety. We found out several days later that the skipper of the PG put himself in for a Medal of Honor. I was livid and put our crews in for Silver Stars, since we saved the SOB's ass. Needless to say, the wise medal writers in Saigon downgraded all of the medals. Our crew received single action air medals, which was appropriate, and the skipper of the PG received a Bronze Star.

We had an unwritten rule: no matter how hot the zone was, we didn't leave anyone behind. No one wanted to get captured and suffer atrocities under the Viet Cong. We would also make sure after we had evacuated everyone that we rolled in and destroyed the downed helo. The Viet Cong had just started using A-37 wire-guided rockets in our area. They would lock onto us from the ground and fire the rocket. It was extremely powerful and very accurate. We were able to eliminate it, if we heard it. If there was a loud buzz and hissing in our headset, we knew that they had a lock on us. We then could fly erratically and theoretically avoid being hit. Fortunately, there were not a lot of them being used in our area, and no one was hit during my tour. However, we lived in fear that they were out there and might be used more frequently. That's what we needed in our daily lives, a little more stress and consternation.

With the enemy activity increasing, the PBR's were asked to extend their patrols to 16 hours, which meant our scrambles increased three-fold. We were flying three and four times a night. We were called out one night to help both the PBR's and the SEALs who were both in a world of shit in the same area. We brought some additional SEALs to drop off to help the others. I landed in a clearing and let the SEALs off. I flew in a shallow arc to cover the SEALs and I could see that they were taking an incredible amount of "incoming" from all directions. We rolled and let the Viet Cong have it from anywhere we saw muzzle flashes. Between the Sea Wolves and the SEALs, we terminated 60 Viet Cong. The next day, after the skirmish, we debriefed with the SEALs over a few drinks. Our version of Father Mulcahey had brought us a case of Filipino rum he had gotten on his R&R. (I doubt that he went for I&I. Well, maybe the first I!) The debriefing turned into a wild party. We were all thankful that the previous day was over and we were not looking forward to the next day's battles.

As activity was picking up, we were told several divisions of Viet Cong were being moved down from the North. How in the hell they moved that many people without us seeing them, I'll never know. Besides living underground, the Viet Cong could hide anywhere. Even the jungle that had been defoliated with Agent Orange was hiding Viet Cong villages. These areas were completely gray. The Viet Cong would build huts and camouflage everything with the gray wood. The only time we could spot them was if they had built a fire or if the SEALs stumbled on them. I often wonder what the cancer rate is among the people who lived like that. Somewhere in my memory, I can't remember which tour it was, I can still see the bomb craters that the B-52's made in these places of devastation. The holes, like mole holes, stretched for miles, one right after the other. The destruction we left in our wake was indescribable. It obviously did great psychological damage to the natives. But not enough, since the war was still going strong.

Every time we returned from a mission, we passed a certain Viet Cong village. It was fairly inactive, but there was a kiln in the middle of it, used by the locals to fire pottery. We used to unload our remaining rockets on it, but for some strange reason, we could never hit it. The rockets would go astray every time, no matter how low we flew or how close we got. It was almost as if there was a force field around it. It grew into a kind of game, but we were never able to hit it.

We were coming back from a mission one day and were about to roll in and try to destroy the old kiln when someone inadvertently hit a water buffalo. The last time I saw that much blood was the night we were under mortar attack in the rice patty. Although some of the other military branches and even some of our own people thought it was great sport to shoot the water buffalo, I never allowed anyone in my detachment to do that dastardly deed. What destruction we had already brought to the country!

It was not long after this incident that I killed my first Viet Cong. We were out on a nice, quiet, sun-lit day patrol, flying over a large, brackish bay way down south in the delta. We saw a sampan with about eight people, and all of a sudden they opened fire at us. These people must have known that they were on a suicide mission. They had to have known the amount of damage we could inflict on them compared to what they could do to us. I didn't wait for clearance to fire from the palace guard. It doesn't make sense to call someone who is many miles away from the action, in a concrete building with no windows, and ask them if the people who were shooting at us were the enemy or not.

So, we rolled in and started shooting our mini-gun. Within one pass, we had killed everyone in the boat. Several of the people fell into the water, and it immediately turned bright red with blood. As we flew away, I became overwhelmed with depression for what we had done. It becomes easier to kill when someone is trying to kill you. We knew that the ones we had killed were Viet Cong, but we usually never knew who the enemy was. This incident added to the list of my recurring dreams affected by my Post-Traumatic Stress Syndrome. It always ends the same way, the pool of red water surrounding the boat in the brown water bay and bodies floating in the murky water.

CHAPTER SIX

We were sitting around, playing Risk and waiting for the next scramble, when all of a sudden there were incoming mortars. It was so intense we couldn't get to the helos, so we dove for the bunker. We always kept shotguns in the bunker loaded with rock salt so we could shoot the rats. The mortar attack went on for hours, and were spaced just far enough apart so that we couldn't make a run for the helos. We had pretty much reached the max kill of rats for the night, so we quietly waited out the raid. The mortar attack was soon over, but I still couldn't stop thinking that the Viet Cong were outside the door waiting to take us prisoner once we exited the bunker.

My Navy training involved attending Survival, Evasion, Resistance and Escape (SERE) School in San Diego. We arrived by bus to a camp in the mountainous foothills outside the city. After a day of school, they turned us loose for a week in the boonies. All we were allowed to have was a knife and the bright orange flight suit on our backs. The idea was to get from point A to point B without getting captured, as well as being able to survive for a week. We were taught how to eat cactus and other supposedly edible things. The trick was to skin the cactus so that all the needles were removed. It was an impossible task, so we all had needles in our tongues and were miserable for several weeks afterwards. Forever, permanently, I struck cactus from my diet. We did capture some rattlesnakes and fried up some snake meat. The snake wasn't all that bad It was particularly good after not eating for a couple of days. The instructors (whom we were to consider "the enemy") pretty much left us on our own until the last couple of days when they pressed hard to capture us. We were pretty easy to find in our orange flight suits. I knew I was captured when they threw me to the ground and put a bayonet to my throat while shouting obscenities at me in Vietnamese. Obviously they weren't playing games. They marched us for miles to a fenced compound where we were stripped down to our skivvies and searched. Earlier, I had taken the watchband off of my watch and hid the face on a safety pin in my skivvies. As a result, I was the only one who knew what time it was. After the search, they hosed us down and we got dressed. We thought back then that a week-old flight suit smelled bad; little did we know that we would be wearing one for up to six months in Nam. While we were in the compound we were on work detail, painting rocks, sweeping dirt, and cleaning the cleanest compound in the world. Somehow, I was elected to be the Chairman of the Escape Committee. The problem was that everyone wanted to know what time it was. A group would huddle around me and I would go for my fly to check it for the time. The enemy figured out that I must be the Chairman of the Escape Committee, since everyone was always huddling around me. While we were in the compound, they played the Communist Manifesto as loud as they could over the loud speakers. I didn't listen to the manifesto but knew it almost by heart after the captivity exercise was over.

Some exercise it was. Although they almost didn't lay a hand on us, we were beaten up pretty badly and badly bruised. Even though we hadn't really eaten in a week, we didn't feel hungry. When it was my turn to be interrogated, a guy with a machine gun escorted me to the interrogation room. On the way, I saw a hole in the fence. I thought I would give it a try, so I jumped for the hole and my escort shot me. They were only blanks, but it felt like I had bullet holes all over my chest. And that is as close to really being shot as I care to get. They put me in the black box, which is just big enough for a body all humped up and bent in thirds. Your chin and chest are pushed down on your bent and aching knees. Several people died in the boxes from suffocation, so they had the boxes on a tilt and came by every ten minutes and had you yell to verify that you were still alive. This was the worst experience I have ever had. After an incredibly long period of time, they let me out and brought me to the interrogation room. As I stepped out of the box, I fell down because my legs had fallen asleep. With them pushing, I staggered into the interrogation room. In school we were told to only give our name, rank and serial number. The interrogator called my wife and children by name and told me all sorts of horrible things they were doing. These guys were obviously not kidding. They were playing for keeps and had done their homework. I can see how people break and give up all sorts of information. They had correctly guessed that I was the Chairman of the Escape Committee, but they never did figure out that I had the watch. It really didn't matter what time it was, though. They pushed me around and slapped me repeatedly until I thought my head was going to come off. It was at that point that I made the decision that no one would ever capture me alive. Living with that thought during all three of my tours in Vietnam, I knew that I would do myself in if I got captured.

After too many hours to remember, they let me go back to the compound. It was dark and getting cold. The enemy started cooking a big pot of something. It smelled good. I was thinking anything would taste good after not having eaten anything but fried rattlesnake and cacti for the past week. We all lined up when they said we could eat. My turn came and I looked into the pot. It was fish heads and rice. The eyes of the fish heads were looking straight at me and I couldn't pick up the fork, the smell was so bad. No matter how hungry I was, I couldn't do it. My stomach was welling up and churning. I knew I was really hungry, but I still couldn't do it. Some of the guys tried it but later barfed their guts out. They left the fish heads and rice cooking all night, and the smell got more sickening as the night wore on. We couldn't sleep, it was cold, and everyone kept asking me for the time. They finally shut off the fish heads and rice and started making coffee. The smell was as unforgettable as the residue of the fish heads and rice melded into the coffee.

As the first light started to rise we could still hear the loud speakers blaring the Communist Manifesto. Then, all of a sudden, the sun shone above the horizon, the speakers stopped with a deafening silence, and the gates of the compound swung open. It was over! The escape and invasion course was over! It could not have been more real. All we had to do was worry about real life when we hit Nam. We jumped on the bus and headed for the city. On the way, we stopped for breakfast at Denny's. We all ordered tons of food, but we could hardly eat. When we got back to the schoolhouse we all weighed in. I was standing on the scale when a short fat Admiral came by and said, "Boy, you look good." The Admiral must have been 50 pounds overweight. I should look good, I thought, because I had lost almost twenty pounds. That's a hell of a way to diet. We got into the debriefing room. We were all exhausted, and the last thing we wanted to do was to debrief. We looked around the room and noticed that three of our comrades were missing. Someone asked where they where. We were told that one was in the hospital and the other two had broken in interrogation, lost their wings, and had been reassigned to a place where they wouldn't have to worry about Nam. We had no idea the stakes were so high. But I supposed they would get higher when we got overseas and into the thick of it.

We received word that we were getting a new toy to play with. The thing was called a continuous rod bomb. It was steel and wrapped around a central core which exploded on impact. When the bomb exploded, the continuous rod flung out and cut down all of the trees within a 200-foot radius, thereby making a helicopter landing area. The problem was that it cut the trees down and left a one-foot stump. It was a real thrill trying to land between the stumps. However, we did find a use for them. The bomb played havoc when dropped in the middle of a Viet Cong village. They were very noisy and could be heard for miles around, even above the roar of the helo. I will leave it to your imagination just what kind of damage they inflicted on a crowded Viet Cong village. The continuous rod as it expanded cut the Viet Cong off at the knees. We only used them on mean mothers that the SEALs had trouble dealing with.

Our base camp at Nam Cam was adjacent to a Vietnamese village. As in most parts of Vietnam, there was no way to tell who the enemy was. The base employed some of the natives, but on regular occasions someone would be caught trying to smuggle in explosives. In the evening, when there would be incoming mortars, we could never tell whether they were coming from the village or the jungle. We could never tell who the friendlies were. The Vietnamese people didn't care that the Americans were there in their country. They had been at war with the French for an eternity.

We were called to do some work near the Cambodian border, and before we knew it, we were actually in Cambodia. President Nixon had stated that, "the U.S. was not in Cambodia," and there I was standing right on Cambodian soil (May 12-15, 1970). It was funny, but after you spent a lot of time in the Far East you could tell Vietnamese from Cambodian, Chinese from Japanese. Vietnamese were the smallest and the frailest looking of the different groups. The Cambodians were slightly bigger. The Japanese and the Chinese are completely different, bone structure, eyes, etc. Nowadays, here in the States, unless an individual is pure bred, I cannot tell them apart. Too bad we couldn't tell the Viet Cong from the Vietnamese good guys. Actually, there were no good guys. It was kind of like the time they told us we would never see the coast of Viet Nam. We did a number of things in Cambodia, but none of it was really fighting. It was a strange and eerie place. It was so quiet and so far removed from Nam that it seemed like a million miles away. Anyway, we never talked about what we did there, for that was an unwritten rule. What we did in the field stayed in the field. We did, however, know what the Khmer Rouge and the Montagnards, the hidden enemy in the Cambodian jungle, did.

Later on, I heard that one of the Sailors who worked for me at the beginning of my tour, while I was at the palace guard, was seriously wounded. He had begged the skipper to go on patrol so he could see some action. He must have figured he could get one of those medals that he helped to write citations for. He was an admin type and the skipper would not let him go. The night before he was to go home, he was sitting in the Petty Officers' Club when a loud bang went off. Everyone looked around and this Sailor was on the floor in a pool of blood. Someone in the next building was cleaning a weapon and accidentally fired off a round. The stray bullet went through two walls and hit him in the face. He wound up in the hospital with his jaw wired and had to have extensive plastic surgery. He spent three months in a Tokyo hospital before finally getting to go home. It was a long tour for him, and he didn't even get into combat. Then, to make things worse, he didn't even get a Purple Heart for serving his country because the wound was caused by "friendly fire."

We had a new pilot check on board the detachment. When I saw him, I knew that I was getting old, because he was the son of one of my old Commanding Officers. Well, when a new pilot checked in, it meant that an old one could go home. It was my rule that when a pilot received his orders back to the States, he could quit flying up to three weeks before he left. The only stipulation was that the day he quit, he would say he quit when he returned from the flight, and not before. The reason I made this rule was because every time a pilot said, "Today is my last flight in Nam," it seemed like he would get shot up. One of my pilots was going to get married a few days after he got home. He picked up his helmet, walked out to the aircraft, and said those words. He went on the mission and took a round in the groin. He was calling "mayday" and was inbound. I met the helo and pulled him out of the cockpit. There was blood all over the place, his flight suit was covered with blood and the panel was splattered. I quickly got him to the medics. They stripped his flight suit off. All he could yell was "Oh my God, I am going to get married next week, and I have lost it all." The doc cleaned the blood off and cleaned the wound off. It looked like a 22-caliber bullet had hit him in the fatty part of the thigh. The doc said not to worry; he had not lost anything. That was the very moment that I made the rule, and it worked like a charm. No one was ever hurt again on his last flight.

On occasion, the Sea Wolves would team up with the Army for search and destroy missions. One of my door gunners had the distinction of flying door gunner in one of the Army loaches (we called them sperm, because that's what the little helicopters look like). These particular missions were very dangerous. The loach would fly down low along the riverbank. The Hueys would fly high and out of earshot. When the loaches took fire, the Hueys would swoop in and kill. One of the inherent problems of flying as a door gunner in a loach is that if the gunner is not careful with the M-60 machine gun he can "brass" the tail rotor. In other words, the spent brass shells would hit the tail rotor as they were dispensed from the machine gun. One of my door gunners flew in the jump seat with the Army pilot. The door gunners shot the machine gun "free-hand" so they could effectively cover the helo's six o'clock position. When the enemy fired at the loach, they put up an increasing amount of firepower. The Viet Cong did not realize that the Sea Wolves were close behind and ready to devour them. When the loach was attacked, the door gunner dropped a smoke to mark the position for us. The skill and courage of the Army loach pilot, and the helo's maneuverability, saved their asses more times than any of us care to remember. But it was the door gunners who did so much of the work. The detachment had two primary door gunners who flew with the Army, but every once in a while a few of the others had the opportunity to experience the thrill of virtually hand-to-hand combat with the Viet Cong. The gunners respected the Army pilots as the second bravest of all war heroes, right after Navy pilots.

On Christmas Day 1969, I was assigned to fly a slick and deliver Christmas trees from Saigon to Long Binh. These trees were for the Admirals and the Generals who were stationed with the palace guard in Saigon. In between deliveries, I was to take a Chaplain to 10 different outposts so he could deliver the Christmas Day service. We picked up about fifty Christmas trees along with the Chaplain, and were off on our mission. At the first stop, a couple of guys asked us if those were Christmas trees in the helo. I said, "Yes. Why don't you take a couple?" We proceeded on our mission, and at every stop I gave a few more trees away. I figured these people in the palace guard didn't need Christmas trees as much as the guys in the front lines did. At the end of the day, I had attended church ten times, an all time record for me. The Chaplain got off at the base when a truck drove up and came screeching to a halt. The driver jumped out and asked if we were the helo with the Christmas trees. "We haven't seen any trees," I said, looking down at the pine needles all over the floor that smelled like an evergreen forest in Oregon. The driver just stood there wondering what had happened. We flew away after having done our good deed for the day and felt really good about it. It was our Christmas present to the troops in the field.

An Army spotter plane was out scouting when he found a huge suspected ammo cache. It was located between the southern tip of Vietnam, Nam Can, and the U Minh forest (known as the "Forest of the Assassins"). They were unable to get the Army to check it out, so the Sea Wolves were scrambled to investigate. It was getting dark, and the spotter had to leave, but he gave us the exact coordinates. It was as tall as a one-story building, so we had no trouble finding it. The fire team formed up and we put in a strike with two birds. We had 28 rockets plus the M-60 machine guns and were firing with all our might. The co-pilot, just for good measure, put in M-79 grenades from his side of the aircraft. Then all of a sudden there was a monstrous explosion, so we swung the bird around to get a better look just as another explosion took place. It looked like the size of a small atomic bomb. We had completed the mission and denied the enemy access to the cache. On the way back to the LST, the Ship's Captain told us he could see our tail numbers in the light of the immense explosions.

On this particular mission, we noticed a sampan that looked like it had field gear and documents on it. It had apparently been abandoned on the bank of the river. There were fresh footprints around the boat. The plan devised on the spot was to have the loach insert the door gunner to retrieve the material and the Sea Wolves would cover them. The uniform of the day for the door gunner was tiger striped fatigue top and blue jeans, bandoliers of ammunition, combat boots, and a free hand for an M-60 machine gun. When the pilot hovered the loach, the gunner jumped out. They were both watchful of the triple canopied tree line, looking for Victor Charles (Viet Cong soldiers). As the gunner jumped out, he sank shoulder deep in mud. The pilot hovered the loach closer to the gunner, and he was able to throw his M-60 machine gun into the rear of the bird. The jungle triple-canopy tree line was now a secondary consideration. Being stuck in the mud was a life and death situation, and the pucker factor was exceptionally high. As the gunner struggled to get out of the mud, he became more and more mired in it. He was up to his shoulders and sinking fast. The situation was a classic "fubar," and the gunner was getting very, very nervous; he later told us he could see his life passing before his eyes. The pilot knew that his man was in deep trouble, and he looked at him with that "Oh, shit" look on his face.

With the helo engine grinding away, it was impossible for any verbal communication to take place. They used facial expressions and sign language when they weren't busy using their hands. They both knew what to do instinctively. The gunner grabbed the skids. The pilot tried to pull straight up into a hover and pull the gunner out of the mud. The small bird could lift directly into the air off of the LST, but the helo had to go forward to gain translational lift before getting airborne. This powerful loach should have had no problem accomplishing this task, but having a gunner in the mud was like having a plunger that could not be extracted from a toilet bowl. The rotor wash was spraying salt water and mud all over the gunner and the helo, and this was causing a visibility problem on the front of the windshield. The pilot made several attempts to pull the victim out of the mud, but nothing worked, and he got sucked deeper and deeper. The gunner could hear the helo winding up to its maximum pitch, and this was also not a good sign. They both knew one thing for sure, and that was that neither of them would give up. The tide was beginning to rise, which made matters worse. The gunner knew that by the time he started sucking seawater, the SEALs and the Sea Wolves would be scrambled to save his sorry ass. The gunner was getting tired and his grip was failing. Just as things looked the worst, the pilot started moving the helo forward and his hanging passenger started to rise out of the depths. All of a sudden, the gunner popped out of the mud with a resounding gulp, and he leaped into the helo—muddy, but safe.

On the way back to the LST, they both looked at one another and thought, what a sorry sight! They landed on the LST and the deck crew and a few Sea Wolves met them and couldn't believe their eyes. Here were two people covered from head to toe and a helo covered from main rotor tip to tail rotor in mud. They both descended into the bowels of the ship and found their way to the showers. The gunner picked mud out of every orifice of his body for several weeks.

We took a few days off and went back to Saigon for a little R&R. One night, I had dinner at a place called The Cave. It just so happened that Premier Ky and his wife were also there that evening. They were dressed in black flight suits with white silk scarves. Mrs. Ky was very beautiful, with her dark eyes, smooth skin, small nose and statuesque body. They came over and introduced themselves to us and we had a very pleasant, but short, conversation. We did not talk about the war because there still officially wasn't one. We ordered our meal, and, naturally, had French Onion soup. If there is one thing that the Vietnamese learned from so many years of occupation by the French, it was how to make French Onion soup. It was the best. After dinner, we walked the streets of Saigon, listening to the various sounds emanating from gangways and private residences.

CHAPTER SEVEN

The War With No Name ended for me a short time after that. I returned home and was stationed in San Diego. I pretty much tried to distance myself from everything having to do with the war. Once in a while, I would hear about some of the crewmen I had served with. One of the guys who flew with me finished his tour, got out of the Navy, and went to work for an oil company in Texas flying people out to the oil rigs. He flew into a power line and all hands were lost. What a waste. You put up with all that shit in Nam and you go back to a nice safe job and get wasted because some asshole put a power line in the wrong place. I felt very fortunate that none of the people on my detachment were killed, I thanked God every day for that. Another one of my guys did wind up in a psycho ward after returning home. That is something I will always regret, though I know there probably wasn't anything I could have done to prevent it. All I could do was be the best leader that I could be.

Several months after being home, I received a package from my detachment one troops. In it was a brick from the village kiln we had tried to destroy so many times. It was mounted on a piece of ammo box and the guys had all signed it with personal messages. I found out sometime later that they had inserted with the SEALs and retrieved the brick just for me, which was probably a pretty hairy trick, and definitely done under fire. I was overwhelmed by the gesture, and the plaque hangs on the wall of my office today.

My co-pilot in HAL-3, Lt. JG. Kevin Delaney, who had been Commanding Officer of Jacksonville Naval Air Station in Florida and was later promoted to Rear Admiral, was the guest speaker at the Sea Wolves reunion where the aircrew was awarded their long overdue combat wings. (His speech appears in Appendix Two of this book.) It was awe inspiring, and a great tribute to the men who fought along side of us.

After many years of living in many different areas of the country, I was eventually able to complete a BA, Masters, and Doctorate in Psychology. All in all, it took me 22 years of night school to complete my three degrees. In those days, there was no reciprocity between schools. I would virtually have to amass residency hours to continue on with my degree as I moved around the country and along the continuum of degree attainment. While in school, I was one of two people to be selected for a one year sabbatical to finish my Masters while on active duty. During that year, I was able to finish my Masters and half of my Ph.D. in Psychology.

The transition from military life to civilian life was quick and fortunately, despite the personal things going on in my life, not too traumatic. This is mostly because I had made the decision to just do it and get on with my life. In June 1977, I made up my mind that I would retire on the first of August. I went to my civilian personnel officer, Jessie. He was a retired Chief Petty Officer who had returned as a GS civil servant. He knew the ins and outs of the bureaucratic system like no one else. He said, "Commander, there is no way that you can get through the system and out by August first." He promised me that it was virtually impossible, but then he called in a couple of his markers in Washington, and the deed was done. I was on the street on August 1, 1977. The day of my retirement, the command gave me a very nice ceremony with fellow officers holding their swords out for me to parade under. I slipped into the rest room, put on a civilian suit, came out, and cut my retirement cake. That same day, I finished my Ph.D., got divorced, and was, for the first time ever, without a job. Talk about traumatic events in one's life.

I made up my mind that there were two things I didn't want to do when I got out: fly or sell insurance. I had worked too hard to get my degrees, and I wanted to use them in the appropriate manner. The first job I was offered was selling insurance and flying the corporate airplane for Armed Forces Relief and Benefit Association. They offered me $14,500 a year. I laughed and declined.

After a number of years in the corporate world, a life even more stressful than Vietnam, I decided to start my own management consulting business. I was tired of being downsized and thrust into one horrible situation after another. One of the contracts I bid on was with the Social Security Administration's Department of Health and Human Services Office. I still function as a Vocational Expert Witness for Disability Cases to this day. I was once assigned to appear as an expert witness for a Vietnamese migrant farm worker who was claiming disability. In the room were a Vietnamese interpreter and the claimant's husband, who was sitting behind me. I knew he was an old Viet Cong soldier. As I listened to them speak Vietnamese, all sorts of emotions flooded my body and mind. I told myself, "Be calm, and relax." The case went smoothly and I testified without showing any bias or malice. At the end of the hearing, the judge called me into his chamber and apologized. He said he would never put me through anything like that again. I said I thought I was pretty cool and didn't think I had displayed any emotion, but the judge said that I was visibly distraught. After reflecting on the incident, I knew I had been visibly distraught.

There were a number of incidents that occurred over the years that made me think maybe the war had affected me in a serious way. The first Fourth of July after I got back, I went to a San Diego Padres night game. I was sitting there calmly when the fireworks began, and I broke into a cold sweat as the bright lights and the rockets burst. So many memories came back. In fact, the entire three tours ran through my mind, so I quickly got up and left the stadium.

While working for a major corporation in Atlanta, I had the opportunity to attend a one-day symposium on Post-Traumatic Stress Disorder. At the end of the day, I went up to the leader and told him that not only was I a psychologist, but that I had also served three tours in Vietnam. I did not reveal that I might be suffering from the disorder. The leader said that they were always looking for good volunteers. I left and told myself that there was no way I was going to be a volunteer. I at least wanted to heal myself before healing anybody else, and for a long time, I felt guilty about the decision not to help out. Then I realized that I had the knowledge to help, but I wasn't going to give it away. I had already given too much in Vietnam. It was selfish, but somehow it didn't feel that way to me at the time. It was more like, "You've taken everything from me emotionally, now you want me to contribute my means of making a living as well? No way!" It just didn't seem fair. But after much denial and other methods of escape, I finally accepted the fact that I had picked up a touch of Post-Traumatic Stress Disorder while in Vietnam.

Post-Traumatic Stress Disorder is classified as an anxiety disorder. Diagnosis of Post Traumatic Stress Syndrome requires that an individual be exposed to a traumatic event that involves experiencing or witnessing threatened or actual death or serious injury to others or oneself. This may include physical assault, sexual abuse, serious accidents, natural catastrophes, and combat experience. Three basic symptoms characterize Post Traumatic Stress Syndrome: re-experiencing the traumatic event (i.e., flashbacks or nightmares); emotional numbing and avoidance (i.e., social detachment or avoiding traumatic memories); and autonomic hyperarousal (i.e., hypervigilance and difficulty concentrating).

Survivors of traumatic railway accidents in the mid-nineteenth century exhibited responses similar to Post Traumatic Stress Syndrome. It was called "Railway Hysteria." The traumas caused anxiety, nightmares, and an extreme startle response. Extreme startle response is just what it sounds like. When a loud noise or other stimuli are presented to an individual, they flinch as the muscles respond to the stimuli. The individual overexaggerates the response. This manifests itself in a number of ways: namely, jumping, flinching, or rapid eye movement. Hypervigilance is what you do when you are in a foxhole waiting for the enemy to come over the fence. In the Civil War it was called "Soldier's Heart." That phrase was coined in 1876. The symptoms exhibited by these victims were rapid heartbeat, hypervigilance and extreme startle response. After the First World War, it was apparent that combat men and women were suffering prolonged psychological damage. In WWI it was called "shell-shocked." Therapists believed that fighting men and women had suffered brain damage due to long-term exposure to bombing and gunfire. In WWII they were suffering from "combat fatigue." After WW II and Korea, other symptoms arose from the trauma of war. Besides nightmares and intrusive memories, social dysfunction, alcoholism, and suicide sometimes followed. DSM-II in 1968 did away with the "stress response" and called it "adjustment reaction" to adult life. I guess their thinking was that war was always included in adult life and an "adjustment reaction" was the consequence!

All of these names identify the same disorder just with different tags. Essentially, they all have the same symptoms and are manifested as Post-Traumatic Stress Syndrome. The American Psychological Association in 1952 published the first ever Diagnostic and Statistical Manual of Mental Disorders (DSM-I). DSM-I called these symptoms "stress response." The Psychology discipline, which up until then had no specific names for the different disorders, never categorized or cataloged them. With the advent of the Vietnam War, and so many men and women being afflicted by the disorder, they felt a need to put some order into the confusion of diagnoses. The DSM classifications helped them do that. Following Vietnam, it became clear that the ravages of war exist even decades after the fighting experience.

I am a living example of that revelation. DSM-III in 1980, and subsequently, DSM-III R and DSM-IV in 1984, used the term "Post-Traumatic Stress Disorder." The authors of DSM-IV state that a traumatic event that can lead to Post-Traumatic Stress Syndrome may involve a threat to one's life or physical integrity and a subsequent response of fear. In addition, significant distress and increased arousal, avoidance of things associated with the event, impaired social or occupational functioning, disturbed sleep patterns and threatening nightmares, and failures to process emotional information all manifest themselves in persons with the disorder.

Post-Traumatic Stress Syndrome, then, is not necessarily associated with war, but rather can be caused by any traumatic event—as early railroad workers found out. A death in the family, an accident or some other such event can easily create the same responses. Post Traumatic Stress Syndrome is a "delayed stress reaction" that may surface years, or decades, after the event that initiated it. Ken Moore, a service officer at the VETERANS ADMINISTRATION center in N.Y., describes it this way: "Let's say a therapist meets a 58 year old Vietnam combat veteran and asks him when was it that he fought in Vietnam. The veteran replies, 'Last night.'" This is one way of looking at the disorder. That is, it removes a person from any ordinary conception of time. This perspective has helped therapists treat the disorder, and has allowed them to better understand it. Moore also said, "Many veterans don't want to be labeled or want people to think that they are crazy." He tells them: "No one needs to know other than yourself, the therapist, and the other veterans." Veterans hide the symptoms in many ways: they become immersed in, even obsessed with, work; they abdicate from society; and sometimes they abuse alcohol or drugs.

Once I completed my Ph.D., I wanted to put my mind to work to figure out how psychologists and psychiatrists could treat Post-Traumatic Stress Syndrome patients who were exposed to the trauma of the War With No Name. Group therapy seems to be an effective method, and has been used extensively and successfully. However, there were a number of anti-war therapists who did more damage than they did good. They would make the members of the group admit guilt for actions or atrocities not actually committed in Vietnam. If a group member did not adhere to the group norms and feel guilty, he was ejected from the group. If nothing else, a patient in group therapy can listen to others and realize that he is not the only one experiencing the same reactions.

Dr. Peter Ziranowski, coordinator of the Post Traumatic Stress Syndrome program in N.Y. and Virginia Medical Center, suggests that sufferers of Post-Traumatic Stress Syndrome use "exposure therapy." In other words, they should force themselves to go to a Fourth of July Celebration, if that indeed is a source of uneasiness. I started by watching celebrations on TV and have now graduated to leaving the windows open and allowing the sounds of the Fourth to seep in. I have taken the position of not allowing the sounds to set me off anymore. A great step in my Post-Traumatic Stress Syndrome recovery. Ziranowski says, however, that returning to Vietnam might not be an effective way of treating the disorder, though visiting the Vietnam Memorial in Washington, D.C. might be a very effective way. I personally would never return to Vietnam. It would do me more harm than good, and I would not be responsible for my actions. Exposure therapy may help veterans deal with unfinished emotional business that needs to be dealt with. Post-Traumatic Stress Syndrome is not curable. But, like any chronic disease, you can learn to live with and manage the symptoms in a healthy way.

I still suffer symptoms of the disorder. To this day, just being in the room with a Vietnamese person is more than I can deal with, and it brings back terrible memories. Several years ago, my wife and I were visiting New York and were in a restaurant having dinner. A Vietnamese boy was busing tables. As he moved about the room, I tried to forget that he was there, but all of a sudden he dropped a tray of dishes behind my table. I jumped up, grabbed him, and threw him up against the wall. After being restrained, I finally got my wits and backed off. Luckily, the owner and the kid understood and they didn't press charges.

Ken Moore says, "Dealing with Post-Traumatic Stress Syndrome might be easier if a veteran could go to a mountain top and scream, or throw it all up and get it out of his system," but it is not that easy. Ziranowski says, "Some [veterans] who never had symptoms of Post-Traumatic Stress Syndrome may experience them with age." Advancing age, then, may be a risk factor for vets who were once able to cope successfully. Ziranowski goes on to say that many veterans have unconsciously dealt with Post-Traumatic Stress Syndrome by becoming workaholics. But when time is freed up at retirement, the symptoms surface and they become more vulnerable to Post-Traumatic Stress Syndrome.

In the book Stolen Valor, B.G. Burkett and Glenna Whitley discuss incidents of Post-Traumatic Stress Syndrome. According to the National Vietnam Veterans Readjustment study, 15.2 % or 479,000 vets suffer from Post-Traumatic Stress Syndrome. In addition, another 11 % have partial Post-Traumatic Stress Syndrome. This brings the total of partial or full Post-Traumatic Stress Syndrome suffers to 830,000. In addition, 13 % claimed they received Purple Hearts, when the actual number was 220,000 Purple Hearts awarded or 7 % of the total. Men killed in action who were awarded Purple Hearts totaled 47,000, 10 % of these were multiple awards. Vietnam veterans advocates raised such a furor, that more money kept flowing from the Federal Government for treatment and Veteran centers. There are 21 Veteran Centers across the country. Between the anti-war therapists, the activities, and the fact that a huge number of people were faking Post-Traumatic Stress Syndrome, it became a cottage industry. Therapists and administrators were not inclined to check veterans' records as long as the money kept flowing for grants.

The authors also site case after case where records, service dates, and medals were falsified. There were cases where veterans who had served in Vietnam, but who did not have Post-Traumatic Stress Syndrome, faked being ill in order to get benefits they felt they deserved. Burkett sites a case where a Navy SEAL faked a Medal of Honor for a battle that did not occur.

Burkett and Whitley explain what a bad rap the press gave the Vietnam veteran during the years of anti-war demonstrations. The press would only interview street people or other shabbily dressed individuals, usually in combat fatigues, adorned with medals and a headband. (The headband and the Huey helicopter were symbols of the Vietnam War.) They cite numerous cases where the people had not been in Vietnam, but they talked of their exploits of bravery and atrocities they had witnessed. Because of Jane Fonda and other groups against the war, the Vietnam veteran has taken the blame for atrocities that did not occur and were lied about.

The real travesty though, is when a real Post-Traumatic Stress Syndrome patient gets put into a group with fakes or malingerers. They get disgusted with the BS and quit, thereby denying themselves the treatment they need. Then there are the people who have just abdicated from society and have become irresponsible citizens because it is the only way they know to escape the horror of war. These are the people who I believe can be helped with other kinds of therapy.

I now live in a neighborhood in Charleston, South Carolina. When I walk down the street where I live, I can look across the Cooper River and see the USS Yorktown, whose deck I once stained with my blood. When I first moved to Charleston, I visited the ship and went to where my old room was. It now has pictures and citations hanging on the bulkhead, and the letter of my designation for Officer of the Deck Under Way hangs there as well. My old room where I spent so many terrifying nights is now a museum. I walked the deck and looked for my bloodstain from 35 years ago. I think I found it, and tears welled up in my eyes as all of the memories came back to me. I remembered the crash, the war, and the loss of my roommate who flew into the water one night.

My neighbor across the street from where I presently live once asked me if I had flown helos and if I knew a certain gentleman. When I heard the name, I was startled and replied, "As a matter of fact, I do. He was my roommate on the Yorktown." I pointed down the street at the aircraft carrier. I could not believe the uncanny twist the rest of the conversation took. He proceeded to tell me that my old roommate's son (also a Naval Aviator) had married this neighbor's sister. Just a mile from the ship that I had flown off of, and a generation between roommates! It boggles my mind, these unbelievable coincidences.

I have been struggling with this book for years. Writing has been very cathartic for me, and has helped heal some of the wounds. I had purposely not joined the Sea Wolf Association or gone to any of the HAL-3 reunions. I did not want to remember, and I did not want to know what had happened to my shipmates. Then it occurred to me, as I reached this point in the book, that there were a lot of stories out there that needed to be told. I finally joined the Sea Wolf Association and contacted some of my old shipmates. The phone calls I received stirred up a lot of emotions and brought back memories, both good and bad. I then decided to complete this book with some of these stories. Two of my door gunners who served with me were at the reunion. They got in a discussion with my wife and expounded on my leadership skills when I was in charge of the detachment. They told stories of incidents that occurred and gave me kudos for leading them through a maze of hard and confusing times. As I listened, I welled up with emotion at the wonderful things they said about my capabilities. Apparently, unbeknownst to me, I did a job that kept us all alive and contributed a great deal to the success of our mission in the War With No Name.

It is my belief that what I have done with my life is to manage the symptoms of Post-Traumatic Stress Syndrome as well as I can, and live a responsible life. This has enabled me to live in reality and be a reliable person. In this book I have tried to relate my experiences and the experiences of others as they related to this war. By opening myself up again to some of these emotions, I have been able to purge some of them from my system. My hope is that by telling this story as I saw it unfold, it will teach others not to abdicate from life. We should realize that we are not crazy, and that we have to learn to deal with the emotions that came from this disgraceful and despicable war.

APPENDIX ONE

The following is the genesis of a theory that I have been working on for a number of years. It is called "responsibility therapy," and may someday be used to treat Post-Traumatic Stress Syndrome and related mental disorders that occur because of a traumatic event. This theory was developed after I finished my education in psychology, and when I realized the relationship between responsibility therapy and Post Traumatic Stress Syndrome.

Studies have shown that 81.5% of the population (Srole, et al., 1962) is somewhat emotionally disturbed, which means that the 18.5 percent remaining make up the bulk of humanity. Is it in the realm of possibility that some of the 81.5 percent could take responsibility for not being mentally ill? There is no doubt in my mind that this could be the case. In my opinion, humanistic psychology is not built on reading, writing and arithmetic. The foundation is responsibility, which diagrammed hierarchically looks like this:

Responsibility

Reality   **Reliability**

Responsibility is what makes people function in reality and become reliable citizens of the earth. Webster, et al., defines responsibility as follows: (1) the state or fact of being responsible; (2) instance of being responsible; (3) a particular burden or obligation upon a person who is responsible; (4)

something for which a person is responsible; (5) reliability or dependability; (6) answerability; (7) accountability. Man's most intrinsic quality is *responsibility*, which is the core of this therapy. I strongly believe that some mental illnesses are a conscious decision to abdicate the position of responsibility. When a person has no sense of purpose, he follows the path of least resistance, becoming apathetic, neurotic and eventually psychotic. Immature or undisciplined people are dominated by emotion. There are some people who truly believe that if they don't do anything, they won't fail. They also feel at the same time, or all of the time, that it is better to decide *not* to decide. For those people who choose to escape from responsibility and reality, there is always intoxication, drugs or suicide.

Every individual is responsible for his own behavior. The therapist should never take responsibility for the patient's behavior. If a person has abdicated their responsibility and chosen to be mentally ill, they must somehow be brought back to reality. They must take hold and nurture the responsibility of their actions back to a healthy position. There will never be any change in a patient's behavior unless he accepts the fact that he alone is responsible for it. It should not be a struggle, as it is to some, to behave in a responsible manner. A person must be creative in his own environment, and he must be responsible for his reality in the sense that he can either let it come to a standstill or actively change it. External influences *do* affect the situation, but they are *not* the ultimate determining factors.

The responsible position in life should be accepted within the mentally healthy position, and within the framework of reality. Once again, it should not be a struggle, as it is to some, to behave in a responsible manner. In order to function in reality, we must first learn how to act responsibly. I agree with Glasser that a responsible person does that which gives him a feeling of self-worth and a feeling that he is worthwhile to others. I strongly believe that a person who doesn't get off of his backside loses it, which is theorized in the evolution discussion. I also agree with Glasser that "people do not act irresponsibly because they are ill; they are ill because they act irresponsibly." For example, an alcoholic or drug addict acts irresponsibly to deny reality and escape it. People who are mentally ill deny reality (Glasser 1965). The underlying assumption to responsibility therapy is similar to Glasser's reality therapy in that we must direct the client toward more responsible behavior which is reality oriented, so that person can be a functioning, reliable person in society. The therapist must guide the client to make a commitment, a concrete decision to act responsibly and give up the ways of irresponsibility. Unlike psychiatry, we must not concern ourselves with the archives and the cobwebs of the past. It is not important how we got there, but it is extremely important to find out what we should do to stay here in reality, be reliable, and act responsibly.

What can we do to give our lives a responsible base so that we can become reliable citizens with a reality orientation? Well, we can first make the decision to act in a responsible manner. Ken Kesey's book, One Flew Over the Cuckoo's Nest, which was turned into a popular movie, is a classic example of a person making such a decision. It is an excellent portrayal of psychiatric patients making the decision to act irresponsibly and choosing the mentally ill position to cope with reality.

Some people fail at choosing to be mentally ill. Could it be that when they make the decision to be mentally ill, they fail because of paradoxical intention? Freedom to choose, and to make a responsible decision, makes man a spiritual being. If the therapist wishes to foster his client's mental health, he should not be afraid to increase the burden of the client's responsibility to fulfill the meaning of his existence (Frankel, 1967). This should also be the case in raising children. As a child grows older, the child should gradually take responsibility for his behavior so that he is fully responsible at adulthood.

Shostrom believes the shift in responsibility for a child's life occurs around eleven or twelve. The responsibility level should be equal between the child and the parent. As the child becomes older, the responsibility shifts to them for their own behavior. In the case of the child, responsibility is difficult to learn, for it is outside the younger child's control. Young children must have frequent reminders if they are to learn responsibility. In short, children have to gradually be taught responsibility from an early age (Shostrom 1967).

The person who rejects awareness, spontaneity, and intimacy also rejects the responsibility for shaping his own life. To make a responsible decision, we must also consider the fact that this decision must be a realistic and attainable one (i.e., an alcoholic who makes the responsible decision to quit using alcohol cannot be successful if he is in the middle of a traumatic experience or exposing himself to a social environment with his drinking buddies every night after work). We must set ourselves up for a win/win situation and not a win/lose or a lose/lose situation.

The alcoholic who is still drinking and the person who has chosen to be mentally ill are both setting themselves up for failure. The alcoholic must make a realistic commitment to quit drinking and take responsibility for his or her behavior. If that person takes responsibility for his behavior, he will be rewarded by an ever-increasing sense of strength, competence and security. Complete identification with oneself can only take place if a person is willing to take full responsibility for his or her actions, thoughts, and feelings, and by ceasing to confuse responsibility and obligation. Some people believe that responsibility means "I put myself under obligation to you." Under no circumstances does it mean that. You are responsible for yourself and your behavior, and I am responsible for my behavior and myself. If a patient decides to act irresponsibly and commits suicide, then it is *his* responsibility, not yours. If the individual chooses to be mentally ill, then it is *his* business until that behavior infringes on society in a harmful way. Responsibility is not a given way to behave, but an unavoidable must. We, as citizens of the earth, are the responsible doers of whatever we carry out. The only alternatives we have are either to acknowledge responsibility or totally deny it. I am not totally in agreement with the position existentialists take when they say, "We are not only responsible for ourselves, but we are responsible for what becomes of others." This school of thought believes in existential anguish, which is what a person feels in bearing the burden of responsibility for all mankind. It is the realization that in making a responsible decision for themselves, they have chosen the position which is sought after by most of mankind (Kapin, 1961). A person is free and well when he accepts the responsibility of his choices. Therefore, if he is oriented to reality, he must choose whatever is in his own best interests.

The patient is the one who changes his attitude toward his fears or other problems, and therefore cures himself of them. This focuses the responsibility on the patient and prevents him from becoming dependent on the therapist. The patient must detach himself from the neurosis. The ultimate goal of responsibility therapy is that the patient should be able to learn to make responsible choices and decisions. Patients should grow in their awareness of their ability and responsibility to cope with a situation in a reality-oriented way. It is my opinion that 81.5% of the population would not be mentally disturbed if we taught responsible behavior at an early age. What happens if this is done at an early age, but the training is interrupted by a traumatic event like war? Then the responsibility training has to be accomplished again so the individual can learn that he should not abdicate his responsible position in life. Responsibly can be learned at any age, however, it is easier to learn correct behavior initially than to overcome previous bad learning (Glasser, 1975). Glasser further states that responsibility should be learned early at home and in school rather than from a therapist. Responsibility fosters mental health and irresponsibility fosters mental illness.

People in our society today do not realize the importance of responsibility and the role it plays in their lives. They think that it comes naturally and easily, and can be turned on and off. This perverse feeling about the nature of responsibility, I believe, is the genesis of mental illness. Persons who do not learn responsibility or do not accept it are the ones who, in prisons or mental institutions, are punished twice as much. Glasser says this because that person had it in his power not to get drunk.

Aristotle says, "Man is responsible to himself for being unjust or self-indulgent." This is true because he has the power not to be that way (Glove 1970). Therapists sometimes consider it pointless to treat persons who have chosen to abdicate the responsibility of life. Who is morally responsible, the abdicator or the therapist? As I have said earlier, the therapist should not take responsibly for the actions of the patient. The therapist *does* have a moral obligation to serve the patient in the best way he can, but he *cannot* in this case.

Therapists and patients alike do not always teach responsibility. The therapist may tell his psychotic patient that he must keep his room clean. If he doesn't do it, the therapist shrugs it off; if he does, the therapist expects it. The parent acts in the same manner; therefore, in either case, responsible actions are not taught and reinforced. We do not set high enough expectations for ourselves, or for others, for that matter. We become lackadaisical in our daily lives, which encourages irresponsible behavior. F.H. Bradley states the position that there is a logical link between the ordinary man's concept of responsibility and the liability to punishment. He says that, for all practical purposes, we need not make a distinction between responsibility, or accountability, and liability to punishment. Where you have one you have the other, and where you don't have one, you don't have the other (Glove 1970).

I agree with Laing et. al. that a good deal of schizophrenia and Post-Traumatic Stress Syndrome is simply nonsense—prolonged filibustering to throw dangerous people off the scent and to create boredom and futility in others. The mentally ill patient is often making a fool of both himself and the therapist. The patient is playing at being insane to avoid, at all costs, the possibility of being held responsible and accountable for a single coherent idea or intention (Laing 1965). Jung confirms this with the statement that the schizophrenic ceases to be schizophrenic when he meets someone who he feels understands him. When this happens, most of the bizarre behaviors, which were taken as signs of the disease, simply disappear (Laing 1965). We expect people to act crazy in a mental ward, they conform to that behavior. Laing argues that the behavior of schizophrenics is generally an intelligible response to the world as they see it, and that their actions are at least as rational as the actions of more normal people (Laing 1965). In addition, Laing argues that schizophrenic behavior is a natural response to certain types of human situations which have resulted from contradictory demands made upon people by their relationships with others, especially members of their families. He describes the schizophrenic experience as a "voyage into inner space and time." He says that we no longer can assume that such a voyage is an illness that has to be treated. This is just another way to abdicate responsibility and escape from the reality of this so-called normal world. American society today uses all sorts of ways to escape. Our society is a drug-oriented society. Just watch television and see what the commercials tell us, not to mention MTV and shows like Survivor. We use alcohol or drugs or whatever it takes to take our voyages. Seems to me, if we learned responsible behavior, we would not want to escape. There are so many things that have to be accomplished in such a short time.

If we keep a reality-oriented base for our lives, we could deal with the trauma that comes with daily living. We would not have to live a life filled with irresponsibility. We beat ourselves down when the first failure comes along, then we look at what a failure we are and choose to make ourselves depressed and anxious. In order to live a full and happy life, we must not feed our neuroses. We must stand up to these feelings of inadequacy that we harbor within ourselves, and not use them to perpetrate the hoax that we are not mentally healthy.

We must choose to be mentally well; we must take the course of responsible action in order to complete the difficult task of living in a chaotic world where most people choose the path of irresponsibility. If we cannot do it ourselves, we must ask for help. First, we have to recognize the fact that we need help. This is the difficult part, but it can be identified by paying just a fraction of attention to our lives. I realize that even when we set out with this goal in mind, the process may be interrupted by inattention, poor communication, a traumatic experience, divorce, or even another War With No Name. This is when, as soon as possible, an outsider should intervene, and another adult or a therapist should take over the process of teaching responsibility. If there is not an intervention for some time, the situation will deteriorate as the person takes on the irresponsible position. He will choose to no longer cope and he will abdicate his responsibility by escaping from reality. As Tillich writes, "Neurosis is the way of avoiding non-being by avoiding being," or in my words, not taking responsibility for our behavior. The process may be slow or rapid, but it can be interrupted at any time. In the early stages of neurosis, a person sets himself up for failure. He consistently tells himself, either consciously or subconsciously, that he is depressed and anxious. The recovering alcoholic who has been sober for some time knows that all he has to do is take the first drink and he is off on the path to destruction. Sometimes he rewards himself for being so good and living a model life. In any case, seethe sets himself up for failure by choosing the path of least resistance and irresponsible behavior. People who commit suicide have set themselves up for ultimate failure, as evidenced by the fact that most tell no less than ten people before they do it.

Once a sound, responsible base is established, growth can occur in one's life. Hierarchically, the next step is reality orientation, which leads to continued mental health and builds a reliable person. I believe that there are three main thrusts to responsibility therapy: reality, responsibility, and reliability. In order to be responsible you must live in reality and be reliable. In order to be reliable, you must choose to act responsibly and live in reality. In order to live in reality, you must act responsibly and be reliable. If we choose not to be responsible, we cannot live in reality and we cannot be reliable or be counted on to be a responsible citizen of the world.

It is my opinion that a number of Vietnam veterans have abdicated their responsibility and have chosen to opt out of life. They refuse to take responsibility for their actions. They escape by becoming dependant on drugs or alcohol. Some have become street people and some have chosen to be mentally ill. When we were young and thought we were invincible we chose an irresponsible position in life. In order to cope with the stresses of the War, we drank alcohol on our days off and did speed on the days we flew. Most of us recovered from our irresponsible behavior. We managed not to do any damage to either ourselves or anyone else and were able to fight and maintain a reasonable daily position in a hellhole. Most of us have come to live useful and productive lives. Some didn't recover and chose to live in another reality, to become unreliable citizens, and to not take responsibility for their lives. What we must do to treat a Post-Traumatic Stress Syndrome patient who is not malingering is to show them the reality of the existence that they have chosen. We must help them choose a responsible position in reality and become a reliable person. How do we do that? It is a question of retraining the individual to learn responsibility again in his life. We must deprogram the sights and sounds that were acquired from participating in the war by either desensitizing or exposure therapy. The individual must force himself to go to fireworks at a Fourth of July celebration, desensitizing the mind to the loud noises and the individual from both the loud noises and the bright lights. We must transform the celebration of the Fourth of July into a celebration, and not a firefight in the jungle in the middle of the night. As the world becomes smaller and there are more Vietnamese immigrants into the United States, we must learn to assimilate our thoughts to the present day and not think of our involvement with these people years ago. We must teach the Post-Traumatic Stress Syndrome patient to learn to accept the here and now, how the world is in its present state, and *not* how it was thirty years ago in the jungle.

As I see life's continuum, from a historical perspective, I find that each of us makes the decision to be a lost soul or a responsible person in our society because we all come with our own historical perspective. Where did we come from? How did we live? When we're put in a particular time and place, we live through the circumstances of life. We then make decisions whether to go to college or go to the military or become a draft dodger. We sometimes have no control over these decisions, and we are asked to join the military. The results of these decisions change the course of our lives. If we found ourselves in a War With No Name, then we must deal with how this trauma affects us. We can choose specific actions and behaviors, ignore the trauma, or let it affect our lives us. The consequences of our actions could be alcohol, drug abuse, or mental illness.

We must make a decision at this point to either abdicate and become mentally ill, or act responsibly. The therapist must reintroduce the concept of taking responsibility back into the life of the Post-Traumatic Stress Disorder patient. When he chooses not to abdicate, he then can live in reality and become a productive and reliable citizen. These concepts are interwoven and perpetuate mental health.

I would hope that these ideas will open some doors and foster some thought concerning another way of looking at mental health and well being as it relates to the Viet Nam veteran and Post-Traumatic Stress Disorder.

APPENDIX TWO

The following is a speech given by Rear Admiral Kevin Delaney at the Sea Wolf reunion in Jacksonville, Florida, in 1998. Kevin was a Lt. JG., Lieutenant Junior Grade (1st Lt. Army and Air Force), and one of my co-pilots in 1969 in Vietnam. At the reunion, we honored the Aircrew men who served in Vietnam as door gunners. The Admiral's speech was dedicated to these unsung heroes who were awarded their Navy Combat Aircrew Wings some 25 years after the war.

"Good evening! What a great pleasure it is to host the Sea Wolves of HAL-3 in a city that has been home to so many of us while we served on active duty, and in a city which truly appreciates our military men and women like no other I've seen-Jacksonville, Florida.

"I would like to think that this has been the year of the HAL-3 door gunners and, without question, this has certainly been the week of the HAL-3 door gunners, and what a great week it has been! Filled with so much emotion, for so many of us, as we proudly recognized those brave men who were the very heart and soul of our squadron and who, in many instances, are responsible for the rest of us being here tonight. The aircrew who so proudly and heroically served as our door gunners. The aircrew who now so proudly wear the wings of a Navy Combat Air Crewman, in the very finest traditions of every Navy and Marine Combat Air Crewman who has ever put his life on the line, to fight for freedom's cause. Truly, these were HAL-3 door gunners, and they still are America's unsung heroes who gave so much and who asked for so little in return.

The battle to get them the recognition that they so richly

deserved was indeed a long one, but one well worth fighting for. And our perseverance has ultimately paid off as we have finally won that battle! I know that I shared your pride in seeing 68 members of our squadron formally recognized on Thursday afternoon with the awarding of Navy Combat Aircrew Wings by our beloved leader, Admiral Elmo Zumwalt, who traveled to Jacksonville specifically to recognize their heroic service to our great Navy and to our wonderful country.

"I know that we all had a tear of pride in our eyes as we honored our shipmates and friends, the Sea Wolf door gunners of HAL-3. And what a fitting tribute it was to also pay very special homage and respect to those Sea Wolf Air Crewmen who made the ultimate sacrifice. They were our brothers and they gave their all to a cause worth fighting for. Because of them, we are here today and I'm sure each of you, like me, has asked yourself a thousand times, 'Why them and not me?' Scripture tells us that 'greater love has no man than this: that a man lay down his life for his friends.' These men were my friends, and they were your friends. These Sea Wolf heroes represent the very bedrock upon which this great country was founded. And it is because of selfless heroes like them, and like you who are here tonight, that our country and our precious freedoms endure and flourish.

"I know that so many of you were as moved as I was during our ceremony at Patriots' Grove-a place of very special significance, which is dedicated to the 80 brave Navy men who, since 1940 (the year of NAS Jacksonville's establishment), have received our nation's highest recognition of Veterans valor, the Congressional Medal of Honor. That award was given to several who served with us on the rivers, and in the jungles, of Vietnam and I am proud to say that the Sea Wolf Association has sponsored one of the seven groves in this very special place of honor. Near the ceremony's conclusion, chills of pride and solemn remembrance came over me as Petty Officer Bugay sang the Navy Hymn and as a flight of our Navy's newest helicopters flew overhead, flawlessly executing a salute to each and every one of you, and then, as a 21 gun salute was rendered and Taps was played to particularly honor our 43 fallen comrades. What a fitting tribute to them, to our squadron, and to all brave Americans who, over the course of our Nation's history, have made the ultimate sacrifice in the service of our great country.

"'In the service of our country.' That really says it all so very well. 'In the service of our country' because that's exactly what the honor of wearing the Navy uniform is all about: Service. It's about trying to make a difference, and it's about taking care of people. Service.

"In Vietnam, the politics of our presence there really wasn't an issue for any of us who had chosen to answer the call. Somehow, 'political correctness' didn't really carry much water for those of us who were serving on the river, in the jungles or in the skies of a far away place called Vietnam. In Vietnam, the politics of our presence really wasn't much of an issue for those of us who had chosen to answer the call.

"In the dark of virtually each and every night, the whispers that would come over the radio, only to be predictably followed shortly thereafter by an all too-frequent cry for help, inevitably came from a friend, a comrade, someone like us, who was simply trying to do his duty.

"Someone who was trying to survive, who looked forward to being one day reunited with family and loved ones. One who was honorably answering the call to service and who was willing to give up his life for his fellow man. It was the voice of a SEAL, a riverboat Sailor, or an Army advisor who knew the real meaning of service and of patriotism, and who, unlike some others, had not run away from that call. It was a call to service which echoed in the ears of so many of us, who joined our Navy in the 60's. It was a call to service instilled in us by our late President Kennedy's challenge for us to 'ask *not* what your country can do for you, but rather ask what *you* can do for your country.' As time passes, I think I speak for all of us when I say that we were truly blessed to have served, at a young age, with truly honorable men who cared so much for their country and for their fellow man.

"Four years ago, when I last had the honor of addressing this group in Pensacola, I recounted a part of our Sea Wolf history. Because many of you and your loved ones were not there, I have been asked to once again recount some of that history.

"After the partition of Vietnam in 1954, the Mekong Delta, and, in particular, the U Mihn Forest, became a stronghold for Vietcong insurgents. Its green fertile fields, triple-canopy jungles, meandering brown waterways and countless tree lines far too often spelled imminent danger for our Navy men who were tasked with keeping the Delta's seemingly infinite canals, rivers and streams open while interdicting communist infiltration through this complex network of waterways. Thus, in this land of hot, dusty, dry spells, and saturating monsoons, when it became apparent that our Navy PBR's would require close air support, Operation Game Warden was inaugurated in December 1965.

"Initially, the Army was tasked with providing helicopters for that purpose; however the Army soon asked the Navy to provide flight crews to fly their 'Hueys,' because our flight crews were better trained in the demanding regime of night and instrument flying, as well as over-water operations.

"The Army helicopters were actually traded to us for some Navy P-2 Neptunes which the Army wanted. Later, as many of you may remember, in a far less official way, Army jeeps were also traded to our Sea Wolf detachments for cases of steaks and lobster tails, which we 'obtained' courtesy of some very creative supply folks at places like Sea Float.

"HC-1 Det. 29 first arrived in the country in July 1966, and the first of several modified LST's arrived at Vung Tau on 11 Nov 1966. We were in business. HC-1's role soon expanded and grew to four detachments that were strung-out throughout the Delta. It soon became apparent that the Navy needed a dedicated gunship squadron with a singular focus on the mission at hand.

"Officially, HAL-3 was born on 1 April 1967. Soon, HAL-3 was growing and there were 9 detachments flying 20 helos throughout the Delta. The DET at NHA BE, DET 2, soon found itself to be the home of many of our former college and high school football players. Because this DET was shore-based and could use a running start and ground effect better, most of the really big guys always seemed to find their way to DET 2. But even though DET 2 pilots and aircrew were generally the biggest guys in HAL-3, there probably isn't a door gunner here who didn't occasionally run along side a struggling, staggering Huey as it groaned and scraped over some P.S.P. [Perforated Steel Plating] and ultimately struggled into the air. Over time, HAL-3's mission grew to include convoy protection, coastal surveillance, agent and sniper insertion, and SEAL support. By mid-1968, the name 'Sea Wolves' was firmly imbedded in the appreciative vocabulary of all our Navy ground forces, and many members of our sister services as well. While most of our pilots were being sent through Huey training at Ft. Benning and Ft. Rucker, there were a few of us 'lucky' ones, who, for fiscal reasons, were sent directly to Vietnam for 'on the job training.'

"Soon, many of us learned that chewing gum or grease pencil marks placed on the cockpit windscreen made far less cumbersome, and far more accurate, rocket sights than those provided by the 'rocket scientists' and bureaucrats in Washington!

"I can't also help but remember those bar glasses that would disappear from all of the bars and clubs in Binh Thuy and Can Tho only to reappear on detachments where they were used as "time fuses" for our unauthorized, but sometimes effective, grenade drops!

"We may have been a wild and crazy bunch of guys, but what a team! To paraphrase Winston Churchill, '*never* have so many owed so much to so few.' Unquestionably, we were a close group. A group that couldn't afford the time it took for the normal maturation process.

"Most of us were pretty young and inexperienced and we had to grow up very quickly. Whatever reservations anyone had about the war, they soon dissipated as we scrambled to save and protect our buddies on the river or in the jungles.

"Because these men were our friends, it soon became a

rather personal war for each of us. Who can forget the first time we medivaced a seriously wounded friend, or carried a body bag containing the remains of a classmate, a friend or a comrade? There was no time to be scared, and we all had a job to do as we headed for our target and engaged the enemy. Only after we were heading home, or after we had landed, did reality set in and afford us the opportunity to think and even ponder the thought of being scared. Most of us were young in age, long on energy, high on enthusiasm, and very short on experience when we checked aboard HAL-3. An average Sea Wolf detachment had a lieutenant commander, and occasionally a CDR, as officer in charge as well as a 'senior' lieutenant (whatever that is) and either a first class petty officer or perhaps one chief petty officer.

"These few 'old salts' were the only 'adult supervision' we had. The rest of our officers were young JG's fresh out of Ellyson Field in Pensacola, proudly sporting brand new shiny wings of gold. I remember at one time we had 128 officers in the squadron and 103 of us were JG's.

"Now *that's* scary. And many, if not most of, our enlisted door gunners had less than 3 years in the Navy. But that didn't stop them from being courageous heroes. Unlike our carrier counterparts, we could never get very far from the action. Living in our bunkers and hooches, it was not uncommon that on our off nights we would grab a few semi-rusted cans of our well-preserved Pabst Blue Ribbon beer, a PRC radio and a rocket box. We'd sit on the rocket box, on top of a bunker or revetment and then tune in the action on the radio as we watched the sky light up with the red and green neon-like stripes of tracers, which were punctuated with rocket fire emanating from overhead Sea Wolf gunships. And rarely was there a night that the Sea Wolves would not be engaged in multiple scrambles. Most often we'd be lying in hot, humid, windowless, non-air conditioned spaces, perhaps partially wearing flight suits and sometimes even our boots, trying to catch a few nods of sleep while waiting for the inevitable whispering voices of PBR Sailors to begin on the radio, knowing that very soon thereafter the call to 'scramble the Sea Wolves' would be heard over the radio. Literally, within seconds, we would be cranking engines and spinning rotors to fly one more time into harm's way, to protect the guys on the river: SEALs who were in trouble, or Army advisors in outposts that were being overrun. The mere word 'scramble' released a flow of adrenaline that energized us all. Whether the call for a 'scramble one' (friend lies in contact), 'scramble two' (U.S. forces in contact), or a 'scramble three' (U.S. Forces in extremis), everyone knew we had a job to do as we ran to man our aircraft. One gunner untied and held the rotor blade, the other held a fire bottle. One pilot cranked the engine while the other strapped in and initiated radio calls. It was not uncommon to be airborne in less than two minutes after "scramble the Sea Wolves" was blasted over our radio. The Viet Cong operated at night, so, of course, most of our most exciting times were in bad weather and at night.

"It was a dirty war in the Delta. As a rule, the Viet Cong took no prisoners and they had no rules. They definitely had never heard of the Geneva Convention or the Red Cross, and there was a price on the head of every Sea Wolf pilot and door gunner.

"The 'Dust Off' helos, flown by our Army brothers, and occasionally co-piloted by some of us, had a red cross painted on the side of their aircraft as a sign that it was unarmed and evacuated the wounded. But instead, that symbol served as nothing more than a large, convenient target for the Viet Cong to shoot at.

"They would steal our ammo and shoot it back at us in their weapons, while *their* ammo was conveniently designed so it could not fit in our weapons. There were no Viet Cong uniforms, and those who professed to be innocent fishermen and farmers by day too often turned out to be our deadly adversaries in the dark of night. It was indeed a very trying time in the United States. We were truly a nation divided against ourselves.

"Vietnam. Here at home, the name alone raised arguments across dinner tables and literally ripped America apart at her seams. In late 1969, when I reported to HAL-3, our troop's strength was at an all time high, with more than 550,000 American service men and women assigned to the Vietnam theater, while, at the same time, 300,000 Americans marched on Washington, to protest our involvement in Vietnam.

"A few months later, in May 1970, the squadron was flying in Cambodia and one of the darkest hours of the Vietnam controversy occurred when four student protesters were shot at Kent State University Ohio by National Guardsmen. But, while dissent had risen to new heights in the states, I must say that some of the greatest unity and greatest friendships were being created and cultivated among our U.S. military men and women who were then serving in Vietnam. Ours was a squadron of brothers bonded by a singular purpose: keeping other Americans, our allies, and ourselves alive! And what an unprecedented job you all did. During the entire war in Vietnam, *no* squadron flew more at night, *or* in the day. *No* squadron flew more combat missions and *no* squadron earned more awards or recognition.

"Let me recount just a few of the amazing statistics compiled by the Sea Wolves of HAL-3:

- Over 78,000 missions
- 131,000 flight hours
- 4,000+ confirmed kills with another 4,200 listed as "probable"
- 6,400 Sampans confirmed destroyed and another 2,300 "probable"
- Over 4,000 structures destroyed and over 5,500 damaged

While exact numbers and some statistics may vary slightly, officially records show that men of HAL-3 were awarded:

- 5 Navy Crosses
- 31 Silver Star Medals
- 2 Legion of Merit Medals
- 5 Navy and Marine Corps Medals
- 221 Distinguished Flying Crosses
- 156 Purple Hearts
- 101 Bronze Star Medals

- 142 Gallantry Crosses
- Over 16,000 Air Medals
- 439 Navy Commendation Medals
- 228 Navy Achievement Medals
- 6 Presidential Unit Citations
- 2 Navy Unit Commendations
- 2 Meritorious Unit Commendations
- 1 Vietnam Meritorious Unit Commendation

"But all of these medals, accomplishments, and triumphs were not without a cost as 43 of our comrades paid the ultimate price in the service of our country. On 26 January 1972, the Sea Wolves of HAL-3 were disestablished, but not before they had forever earned an honored place in the annals of national aviation history and the begrudging respect of the Viet Cong and North Vietnamese Army.

"While America may have pulled out of Vietnam without having finished the job it set out to do, it would be all too easy to dismiss our efforts as futile. For our part, the Sea Wolves saved countless lives and wrote a new, brave, and heretofore unheard of chapter in national aviation history. Communism was contained in Southeast Asia, the cold war was eventually won, and more people around the world now bask in freedom's light than ever before. We were indeed a dominant force in the Mekong Delta, and we rewrote the books with regard to employment of helicopters in reverie warfare. Simply put, the Sea Wolves of HAL-3 have set a benchmark standard which will be hard, if not impossible, to beat.

"And, more than anything else, and clearly most importantly, many of our fellow Americans-our 'shipmates,' in the finest sense of the word-are alive today to tell sea stories to their children and to their grandchildren because *we* were there, answering the call to support those brave Americans who chose to put their lives on the line in the rivers and in the jungles of South Vietnam, in the service of our great country. Let me simply say what an honor it is to be called a 'Sea Wolf' and how much I value the friendships that began half a globe away, over a quarter century ago, in the Mekong Delta.

"In closing, let me slightly modify a quotation from President John F. Kennedy and say, any man who may be asked in this century what he did to make his life worthwhile, I think can respond with a great deal of pride and satisfaction, 'I served with the United States Navy Sea Wolves of HAL-3.'

"Thank you, may God bless you and all of our comrades, especially those who have fallen or are missing, and may God continue to bless the brave military men and women who continue to serve and sacrifice, each and every day, around the world to keep our great country free and ensure that America is always the land of the free and the home of the brave. Thank you."

GLOSSARY

Admiral   Same as a General in the US Air Force and ARMY

Bird   Helicopter or fixed wing aircraft

Captain   Captain US Navy: Same as a Colonel in the US Air Force and US Army

CO   Commanding Officer

C.I.A.   Central Intelligence Agency

DET.   Detachment: Home of a group of Sea Wolves in Vietnam

FCLP   Filed Carrier Landing Practice: An airfield painted like an aircraft carrier and of the same length as a carrier

HAL-3   Helicopter Attack Light Squadron Three (Sea Wolves)

I & I   Intoxication and Intercourse

Loch   A small military helicopter; derived from L.O.H. (Light Observation Helicopter)

Lt. Jg.   Lieutenant Junior Grade: Same as a First Lieutenant in the US Air Force and US Army

Lt.   Lieutenant: Same as Captain in US Air Force and US Army

Lt. Cdr.   Lieutenant Commander: Same as Major in the US Air Force and US Army

LSO   Landing signal officer: The officer stationed at the stern of the carrier on the left side. Their function is assist the pilot in landing the aircraft aboard the Carrier

Lurprats   Long Range Patrol Rations-just add water and you have a meal!

PTSD   Post-Traumatic Stress Disorder

POL   Petroleum Oil Lubricants: the place where helos land to refuel and rearm

PBR   Patrol Boat River: A small boat used to patrol the rivers and to insert SEALs

RESCAP   Rescue helicopter

R & R   Rest and Relaxation

RPM   Rotations Per Minute

SW-16   Sea Wolf One-Six: Officer in charge of detachment one

Tracers   Phosphorous ignited bullet heads on .50 caliber machine guns, present on every 5th bullet so when they are fired you can track your shooting to the target

T-33   Jet training aircraft

VN   Vietnam(ese)

VC   Vet Conga

1. Marine F4-U Corsair, a gull-winged single reciprocating engine fighter plane.
    The F4-U Corsair was the state of the art fighter at the time and was used extensively in Korea. The aircraft with fuel weighed 14,100 pounds, and was fitted with a Pratt & Whitney R-2800 Double Wasp, 18-cylinder, 2200 HP engine. Armament on board was six 50-caliber machine guns. The Corsair had a maximum speed of 395 mph with a ceiling of 37,000 feet.

2. SH3-A Sikorsky Aircraft Division of United Technologies, Stratford, Connecticut, at the cost of $6.4 million, was powered by two General Electric T-58-GE-402 turbo shaft engines. The aircraft was 73 feet long, 17 feet high, with a maximum take off weight of 21,000 pounds, flying range of 542 miles and a maximum ceiling of 14,700 feet.

3. Douglas Aviation built C-54. The aircraft is 93 feet, 11 inches long, the wing span is 117 feet, 6 inches, and the height is 27 feet, 6.25 inches tall. Gross weight is 73,000 pounds. maximum speed, 280 mph; maximum range, 4,250 miles; maximum altitude, 22,300 feet. The aircraft holds three crewmen and 70 passengers. The four engines are 1,450 HP Pratt & Whitney R2000's.

4. Bell Aircraft Tectonics. The aircraft is 31 feet long, 10 feet high. Maximum weight, 3200 pounds; range, 420 statue miles; maximum altitude, 18,900; maximum speed, 138 mph; and capable of carrying two passengers.

BIBLIOGRAPHY

Bradley, F.H. *Collected Works of F.H. Bradley*. Bristol: Thomas, 1999.

Burkett, B.G. and Glenna Whitley. *Stolen Valor*. Dallas: Verity Press, 1998.

Dreamy, Michael F. *Being and Earth: Paul Toilet's Theology of Nature*. Lanham, MD: UP of America, 2000.

Frankly, Victor. *Man's Search for Meaning: An Introduction to Logotherapy*. New York: Pocket Books, 1963.

Glasser, William. *Reality Therapy in Action*. New York: Harper Collins, 2000.

Glover, Edward. *The Technique of Psycho-analysis*. New York: International UP, 1968.

Jung, C.G. *The Basic Writings of C.G. Jung*. New York: Modern Library, 1993.

Kaplin, H.eds, *Social Psychology, the Self-Concept*, Shoestring press1961

Laing, R. D. *The Divided Self: An Existential Study in Sanity and Madness*. London: Penguin, 1990.

Lange, Arthur, J. *Responsible Assertive Behavio*r. Champaign, IL: Research Press, 1978.

Moore, Ken, quoted in *Stolen Veterans Administration*, by B.G. Burkett and Glenna Whitley. Dallas: Verity Press, 1998.

Shostrum, Everett L., Lila Knapp, and Robert R. Knapp. *Actualizing Therapy: Foundations for a Scientific Ethic*. San Diego: EDITS, 1976.

Srole, Leo. *Personal History & Health*. New Brunswick, NJ: Transaction, 1998.

Ziranowsky, Dr., quoted in *Stolen Veterans Administration*, by B.G. Burkett and Glenna Whitley. Dallas: Verity Press, 1998.

ABOUT THE AUTHOR

Art Schmitt was born in Brooklyn, NY. He served his country as a Naval Aviator for 22 years during which time he received The Distinguished Flying Cross, a Bronze Star, 21 Air Medals, 2 single action air medals, Presidential Unit Citation, Vietnamese Cross of Gallantry, and a Vietnamese air medal. He received his Ph.D. from U.S.I.U. in San Diego, CA in 1976. In 1978 he was listed in Who's Who in the West for inventing an alcoholism education game, "Beat The Drinking Game." He was a registered psychologist in California and Florida and licensed Marriage Family Therapist in Georgia, Kentucky and Oregon. Art is a certified flight instructor to the NASA Space Program. He is also certified to teach courses in counseling psychology, organizational development, military science, health and physical care services. Art is a psychologist, lecturer, teacher, author, consultant, and has a commercial pilot's license. He has worked in the corporate environment as a Vice President of Human Resources. In 1988 he established his own business, Business Team Builders, a Human Resources Management Consulting firm. One of his current contracts is with the Social Security Disability Administration where he acts as an Expert Witness. Art is married and he and his wife currently reside in Charleston, SC.

ABOUT GREATUNPUBLISHED.COM

45321523R00092